The People's Choice

The People's Choice

HOW THE VOTER MAKES UP HIS MIND IN A
PRESIDENTIAL CAMPAIGN · By Paul F. Lazarsfeld,
Bernard Berelson, and Hazel Gaudet

Third Edition

Columbia University Press
New York and London

To Frank Stanton and Sam Stouffer
Expert Consultants and Generous Friends
— P. F. L.

Copyright 1944, 1948, 1968   Columbia University Press

First Edition, 1944, Duell, Sloan and Pearce
Second Edition, 1948, Columbia University Press
Columbia Paperback Edition   1968

Library of Congress Catalog Card Number: 68–20443

Printed in the United States of America

Preface to the Third Edition

More than twenty-five years have passed since the first study of the people's choosing. During this period, some of the ideas originating in that study have been slowly nurtured by a group of sociologists at Columbia University; some themes have been taken over and enlarged by colleagues in other research centers. Members of related social sciences disciplines have touched upon our work, sometimes in a critical way. It is our intent to comment upon certain of these developments in the Preface to this new edition.

In the Preface to the Second Edition, too, we intended to stress this idea of continuity. At that time, it seemed essential to clarify the nature of panel studies. Now that panels are an established part of social research procedures, a broader range of developments can be reviewed. For one, certain ideas which are expressed only tentatively in the first report have now been empirically tested. In addition, much of the original data, unanalyzed at the time of the study, has now been mined. We had not the time or money to explore two important topics then: the mutual interaction between several variables and the possible effects of reinterviewing the same respondents. In Columbia's tradition of secondary analysis, the necessary work has been carried out since the original study. We now take this occasion to present it for discussion. At the end of the introduction, we shall try to trace the outcome of some of the promises offered early in the research. We shall see how much of the proverbial "further research needed" as outlined in the Preface to the Second Edition has materialized thus far.

We start with the first topic we mentioned. To what extent have ideas which were somewhat marginal and speculative in the original text been followed up? The final chapter, pages 150 to 157, provides several good examples.

Personal Influence

In the election period of 1940, the role of mass media turned out to be rather small, mainly—as one can speculate in hindsight—because most arguments were formulated either for or against Roosevelt and had become rather stereotyped through the two previous campaigns. Yet, in the course of the study, we were surprised by what seemed to be a great deal of person-to-person interaction, particularly during the critical months. The study did not permit us to document this impression very specifically because our primary efforts were directed toward establishing the role of the more formal media. All we could do at that time was to raise a number of speculations, revolving about the "opinion leaders" we had identified. These people were the interested, highly articulate voters who gave political advice or even tried to convert other citizens. We discovered that these opinion leaders were found in all occupational groups; they were by no means simply the wealthiest or the most prominent people. But, how did they actually affect the decisions of others? Even then we were intrigued.

Although we did not scrutinize the nature of personal influence in the 1940 study, we alluded to the conception of a "two-step flow of communications." By this we meant that the mass media often reached their audiences in two phases. After opinion leaders had read newspapers or had listened to broadcasts, they would filter bits of ideas and information to the less active sectors of the population. This preliminary hypothesis was tested through a special study in Decatur, Illinois, and was reported in a book on *Personal Influence,* by Elihu Katz and Paul Lazarsfeld.[1]

[1] Elihu Katz and Paul F. Lazarsfeld, *Personal Influence*, Glencoe, Ill.: The Free Press, 1955.

Katz continued to explore the implications of the findings. For one, he made a rather disconcerting discovery. The role of opinion leaders was not nearly so revolutionary or unheeded as we had thought. For a long time, rural sociologists had noticed the part played by such intermediaries in the dissemination of agricultural innovations.[2] Katz proceeded to elaborate on this parallel, and he, together with two colleagues, James Coleman and Herbert Menzel, extended the research into a new field: the mode by which physicians adopt medical innovations.[3]

Because of the war, we could not carry out a second voting study in 1944, but many of the earlier speculations were built into a new panel study in 1948, in Elmira, New York. That study was published in 1954, as *Voting*;[4] a chapter entitled "The Social Psychology of the Voting Decision" incorporated what had been learned about the whole decision process.

Not only did some of the substantive ideas from *The People's Choice* take root, but the panel technique itself was subjected to systematic codification. The study of short-time change was organized as a specific series of analyses. The starting point was the turnover table which we explained in the Preface to the Second Edition of this book. But this turnover in respondents' attitudes between one interview and the next can vary among different subgroups of the total sample. Such a "qualified turnover" analysis became a second step in panel research. It was particularly elaborated through the study of people who had intended to vote but did not do so, a topic of practical relevance to the understanding of election predictions. William Glaser has written about this phase of panels.[5] Once the two steps of

[2]Elihu Katz, "The Two-Step Flow of Communication: An Up-To-Date Report on an Hypothesis," *Public Opinion Quarterly*, XXI (1957–58), 61–78.

[3]James S. Coleman, Elihu Katz, and Herbert Menzel, *Medical Innovation: A Diffusion Study*, New York: The Bobbs-Merrill Co., Inc., 1966.

[4]Bernard Berelson, Paul F. Lazarsfeld, and William N. McPhee, *Voting: A Study of Opinion Formation in a Presidential Campaign*, Chicago: University of Chicago Press, 1954.

[5]William Glaser, "Intention and Voting Turnout," *American Political Science Review*, LII (1958), 1030–40.

turnover and qualified turnover were clarified, it was at last possible to develop a full-blown analysis of social process by moving to a third level—how changes in several variables are related to each other. In other words, attitudes not only change over time but, as they shift, one attitude affects others. It is this last step, the study of the mutual interaction of a series of variables, that acquired a life of its own and became dominant in a number of subsequent studies.

The files of *The People's Choice* actually contained the raw material for such an analysis, but the technique was still not available at the time of the second edition. The approach developed slowly until we were able to utilize the early data. We now take this opportunity to include the main results of these "mutual interaction" analyses.

Mutual Interaction Over Time [6]

In 1940, Willkie had emerged as a new political figure, and Americans of various political persuasions were forced to make up their minds about him. Their feeling about Willkie as a person was, of course, closely related to their vote intention. Table 1 contains all the combinations that can be derived from the basic information about voter's intent and attitude toward Willkie in Erie County, Ohio, in 1940. It is known as a sixteen-fold table. One can see that early in the campaign, immediately after the conventions (August), the relation between attitudes and vote intent was not as strong as it was two months later. The number of divergent cases (Republicans against Willkie or Democrats for him) declined from 59 to 42, as can be seen from the totals of Table 1.

If people have a tendency to "harmonize" their attitudes as the campaign goes on, in which direction do they move—do they adjust a specific opinion to their vote intention or does the

---

[6] A detailed analysis can be found in S. M. Lipset, P. F. Lazarsfeld, A. H. Barton, and J. Linz, "The Psychology of Voting: An Analysis of Political Behavior," in G. Lindzey, ed., *Handbook of Social Psychology*, Cambridge, Mass.: Addison-Wesley Publishing Co., Inc. 1954, pp. 1150–64.

TABLE 1: CONCURRENT CHANGE IN VOTE INTENTION AND PERSONAL LIKING FOR WILLKIE
(*Erie County, Ohio, 1940 Election*)

			Second Interview				
		Party	+	+	−	−	*Total*
		Willkie attitude	+	−	−	+	
First	(++)	Republican for Willkie	129	3	1	2	135
Inter-	(+−)	Republican against Willkie	11	23	0	1	35
views	(−+)	Democrat for Willkie	1	0	12	11	24
	(−−)	Democrat against Willkie	1	1	2	68	72
		Total	142	27	15	82	266

process go the other way? The answer comes from the crucial twenty-four cases which are characterized as follows: they are "divergent" at the first interview in the sense that they are not following the majority patterns, Democrats who are for Willkie and Republicans who are against him; but in the second interview they are "in harmony," their opinions and attitudes match. This pattern is as indicated in Table 2. It is seen that the majority of this small but critical group retains its vote intention and adjusts its opinion about Willkie. Party loyalty is more

TABLE 2: THE RESPONSE PATTERN OF PEOPLE WHO HARMONIZE THEIR ATTITUDES BETWEEN TWO INTERVIEWS

		Second Interview	
		++	−−
First	+−	11	1
Interview	−+	1	11

deep-rooted than is the attitude toward a newly emerging political figure. There is another group (shown in Table 3) which deserves attention. These are the people who were in

TABLE 3: THE RESPONSE PATTERN OF PEOPLE WHOSE ATTITUDES BECAME DISSONANT BETWEEN TWO INTERVIEWS

		Second Interview	
		+−	−+
First	++	3	1
Interview	−−	1	2

harmony the first time but, at the second time, revealed a dissonant attitude pattern.

Their shift permits a twofold interpretation. For one, they indicate to what extent the whole process is affected by factors other than the two under study. If the second and third figures in the first and fourth row are large, we will know that extraneous factors affect the relation between the two attitudes even if temporary harmony had been achieved. At the same time, we can see which of the two basic variables is more subject to "shock effect." In the present case, the attitude toward Willkie is less stable than the voting intention.[7]

Analysis of this kind points to a general procedure which formalizes and clarifies the old notion of relative strength or depth of a series of attitudes. From the files of *The People's Choice*, data are available on the following topics: vote intention; personal liking of Roosevelt; personal liking of Willkie; attitude toward the third term; and opinion on the importance of government *vs.* business experience for a president. On these five issues, 10 sixteen-fold tables similar to Table 1 can be set up. The line of reasoning following Table 2 may then be translated into an index to express the "relative strength" of the two variables in each pair. The details of this index will be omitted here; suffice it to say that the index takes into account the stability of each variable separately and that the more change in one variable is influenced by change in another, the larger the index will be.

As was to be expected, each attitude was found to be correlated to a greater or lesser extent with every other attitude in the group. It was also found that all the correlations were higher at the second interview than at the first. As the campaign progressed, the voters developed increasingly consistent attitude

[7]An insightful discussion of such interaction tables has been provided by Donald Campbell, "Quasiexperiments and Research Design," in Chester W. Harris, ed., *The Measurement of Change*, Madison, Wis.: University of Wisconsin Press, 1963. Its mathematical treatment has been considerably advanced in James Coleman, *Introduction to Mathematical Sociology*, New York: The Free Press, 1965, Chapter X.

patterns, adjusting many conflicting opinions to the general pattern. By evaluating an index of mutual effect between the various attitudes, we can determine the relative importance of each of the attitudes in establishing the final pattern.

TABLE 4: RELATIVE STRENGTH OF FIVE ATTITUDES

Strength *	Vote intention	Roosevelt opinion	Third-term opinion	Willkie opinion	Government vs. business experience
Vote intention	—	+.029	+.037	+.129	+.144
Roosevelt opinion	—.029	—	+.052	+.067	+.101
Third-term opinion	—.037	—.052	—	+.025	+.090
Willkie opinion	—.129	—.067	—.025	—	+.079
Government vs. business experience	—.144	—.101	—.090	—.079	—

* In order of strength relative to vote intention

A definite rank order of importance emerges for the attitudes: Each variable is stronger than every variable below it in the chain and weaker than every variable above it. The complex aggregate of attitudes making up party loyalty, and thus vote intention, is more powerful than any single campaign issue. That is, in the 1940 campaign, a person's vote was not determined by his opinion on any one of the specific campaign issues, but his opinions on these issues were instead determined by his party loyalty.

The specific issues connected more or less directly with the person of President Roosevelt were the most important. "Opinion of Roosevelt as a President" was the strongest of any of the attitudes. Following that is "Opinion on the Third-term Question," which was itself determined largely by both "Vote Intention" (i.e., party loyalty) and "Opinion on Roosevelt." "Opinion of Willkie as President" was much less important as we should expect, because Willkie was comparatively unknown.

The basic idea of this kind of process analysis has since been applied to a variety of data and topics. Thus, Rosenberg has studied occupational choices and general values as they interact

during the maturation of college students.[8] McDill and Coleman [9] apply the method in a study of high school students; here
the problem was to see how their social relations and their
academic interests interact. In market research, the interaction
between owning a product and exposure to its advertising has
been studied this way.

One might say that on this point *The People's Choice* provides a bridge between empirical research and traditional concern with the concept of social process. On another point the
panel technique was more on the defensive; this Preface offers
an opportunity to review the matter.

Panel Bias

One question about panel studies troubled us from the very
beginning. Does the repetition of interviews affect the responses?
For example, if one informs a group of people that they will be
successively reinterviewed as to whether they know the geographical location of Saigon, the proportion of positive replies
will rapidly increase. Yet it would definitely be hazardous to
attribute this change to a rising involvement with the war; it
probably merely represents increased acquisition of facts. On
the other hand, it is unlikely that an expression of vote intention
would demonstrate a similar change over repeated interviews.
Probably most of the questions in sociological interviews lie
somewhere between these two extremes. But we could not even
establish the extremes without putting them to test.

We laid the grounds for the test in the Erie County study.
Our basic panel consisted of 600 respondents. In the first wave,
we actually interviewed 3,000 people and formed at random
four groups of 600 each. Each of the three groups who
were excluded from the panel were reinterviewed only once

[8]Morris Rosenberg, *Occupations and Values*, Glencoe, Ill.: The Free Press, 1957.
[9]Edward L. McDill and James Coleman, "High School Social Status, College
Plans, and Academic Achievement," *American Sociological Review*, XXVIII
(1963), 905–18.

more. The timing of the reinterviews is indicated in the following scheme.

		Control Groups		
		A	B	C
First interview	May	*	*	*
Second interview	June			
Third interview	July	*		
Fourth interview	August		*	
Fifth interview	September			
Sixth interview	October			*
Seventh interview	November			

The data resulting from these experiments were later intensively analyzed by Charles Y. Glock.[10] Glock breaks down the rather general idea of panel bias into a number of specific questions which he was able to test with available data. He puts himself into the position of a skeptic who assumed that a reinterview effect would exist and proposes that this could take several forms. Among those specified by Glock are:

a) Reinterviewing will make the panel members more aware of and, in turn, more interested in the topic being studied than they would ordinarily have become.
b) Reinterviewing will produce greater exposure on the part of panel members to information about the topics being studied.
c) Reinterviewing will cause the panel members to resolve conflicts in their own thinking about the topic more quickly than they would otherwise have done.

A typical test case for the first hypothesis would come from a question which was asked in the first, fourth, and sixth waves of the Erie County study: "Would you say that you have a good deal of interest in the coming elections, a moderate interest, a mild interest, or no interest at all?" The testing pro-

[10]Charles Y. Glock, "Participation Bias and Reinterview Effect in Panel Studies," unpublished doctoral dissertation, Columbia University, 1952.

TABLE 5: EFFECT OF REINTERVIEWING
(*In percent*)

Level of Interest in Xth Wave Relative to Interest in First Wave	Fourth Wave		Sixth Wave	
	Panel 4	Control B	Panel 6	Control C
Increased	22	22	34	28
Remained the Same	66	66	58	60
Decreased	12	12	8	12
	100	100	100	100

cedure consisted of comparing the panel and the control group whenever that was possible. The result is reported in Table 5. This is the characteristic form of all the tests carried out by Glock. The table shows that, at Wave 4, the distribution of interest of the panel and the control group was alike although the panel was in its fourth interview and the control group in its second. When the panel was in its sixth interview and the corresponding control group in its second, the interest had increased in both groups. This increase was slightly higher in the panel than in the control group. However, the difference did not appear in other, similar tabulations. In sum, Glock is justified in saying that no evidence of a reinterview effect on interest in the campaign is found.

As to the second hypothesis, that regarding the effects of the interview on exposure, there was a large amount of data available because the study was especially designed to trace the effect of mass media. Between the first and subsequent interviews, both panel and control groups increased in exposure to approximately the same degree. However, it was found that as time went on panel members turned more to radio and less to magazines than did the control groups. It so happens that throughout the study, questions on radio listening were more frequent than questions on magazine reading. This might have directed the panel's attention to the range of radio material available.

The most clear-cut result was obtained on the third aspect selected for this summary. Glock concentrates on the proportion of respondents who had not yet formed a voting decision; it decreased, of course, as election day approached. By comparing panel and control groups, he comes to the following conclusion: because of reinterviewing panel members develop voting intentions more quickly than do members of the population one is trying to sample. (Men were more susceptible than women to this effect.) But, the proportion of Republicans and Democrats was not affected.

In his analysis Glock includes panel studies made subsequently to the present one. A detailed summary of his findings is available in a French translation.[11] There it can be seen how many insights into the experience of panel members can be gleaned from the simple procedure exemplified in Table 5.

Expectations and Confrontations

In the Preface to the Second Edition, we sketched out several avenues of further research. Of the many that actually materialized, three have already been discussed: personal influence, mutual interaction between attitudes, and panel bias.

Although we had suggested a more detailed analysis of the personalities and social backgrounds of people who change during an election, we do not know of any work along these lines. However, a significant variation of such an inquiry has been carried out by Patricia Kendall, who studied in detail the type of questions and situations that led to increased or diminished turnover.[12]

In what we had termed the methodological challenge, we suggested a probing into the relation of the panel method to other disciplines. Since then, Theodore Anderson has applied the mathematics of Markov Chains to our data, and his paper has proved to be seminal for many subsequent mathematical studies of social processes.[13]

[11]See François Chazel *et al.*, eds., *Méthodes de la Sociologie: Analyse Diachronic*, Paris: Mouton, 1968.

[12]Patricia Kendall, *Conflict and Mood*, Glencoe, Ill.: The Free Press, 1954.

[13]Theodore Anderson, "Markov Chains and Panel Analysis," in Paul F. Lazarsfeld, ed., *Mathematical Thinking in the Social Sciences*, Glencoe, Ill.: The Free Press, 1953.

Our early interest in the correlation of panel studies with laboratory experiments in psychology prompted us to invite the late Carl Hovland to attend a summer seminar held in 1954, at Dartmouth College (with the aid of the Center for Advanced Studies in the Behavioral Sciences). His illuminating examples can be found in the address he gave as President of the Eastern American Psychological Association.[14] Bernard Berelson related the behavioral findings of panel studies of voting to political theory.[15]

Quite a number of election studies based on panel techniques have been made in England and France;[16] several have been reviewed by François Chazel.[17] During the congressional elections of 1954, the Columbia group, in collaboration with other members of the American Association for Public Opinion Research, set up a number of regional panels. The ensuing publication shows the adaptability of the technique to varying social contexts.[18] The Free Press meant to include the Columbia voting studies in a series of monographs which they had started

[14]Carl I. Hovland, "Reconciling Conflicting Results Derived from Experimental and Survey Studies of Attitudes Change," *American Psychologist*, XIV (1959), 8–17.

[15]See *Voting*, Chapter 14. Berelson has also developed a systematic list of findings later incorporated in an inventory of social science knowledge; see Bernard Berelson and Gary A. Steiner, *Human Behavior*, New York: Harcourt, Brace & World, Inc., 1964.

[16]See Mark Benny, A. P. Gray, and R. H. Pear, *How People Vote: A Study of Electoral Behavior in Greenwich*, London: Routledge and Kegan Paul, 1956; Foundation Nationale des Sciences Politiques, *L'Établissement de la Cinquième République: Le Référendum de Septembre et les Elections de Novembre 1958*, Paris: Armand Colin, 1960; R. S. Milne and M. D. Mackenzie, *Straight Fight: A Study of Voting Behavior in Greenwich*, London: Routledge and Kegan Paul, 1956; and R. S. Milne and M. D. Mackenzie, *Marginal Seat, 1955: A Study of Voting Behavior in the Constituency of Bristol North-East at the General Election of 1955*, London: The Hansard Society, 1958.

[17]François Chazel, "La méthode du panel et ses possibilités, d'application," *Revue Française de Sociologie*, VII (1966), 684–99.

[18]William N. McPhee and William Glaser, *Public Opinion and Congressional Elections*, Glencoe, Ill.: The Free Press, 1962.

under the title "Continuities in Social Research." [19] The idea of this series was to take a major published study as a starting point and to have various experts comment on its implications for further research and on its significance for related inquiries. So many contributions were offered to the proposed third volume that finally the two editors, Brodbeck and Burdick, decided to publish a more general volume on American voting behavior.[20] Still, several of the articles dealt specifically with panels. We want to draw special attention to Talcott Parsons' effort to link our empirical findings with his general theory of social systems. Ratbush stressed the possible applications of the panel technique to the repeated observation of buying behavior, a type of market research which has since been utilized in many places. Eleanor Maccoby's doubts about the logic of the panel technique are still being discussed in the literature.[21]

I am grateful to the Columbia University Press for this opportunity to sketch out our own continuity.*

Paul F. Lazarsfeld

New York, N.Y.
December, 1967

---

[19]The first two volumes dealt with *The American Soldier* and *The Authoritarian Personality*.

[20]Arthur Brodbeck and Eugene Burdick, eds., *American Voting Behavior*, Glencoe, Ill.: The Free Press, 1959.

[21]Two expository presentations of the panel technique are available. See Hans Zeisel, *Say It With Figures*, New York: Harper Brothers, 1963, fourth edition, Chapter X; and Jiri Nehnevajsa, "Die Panel Methode," in René Koenig, ed., *Handbuch der Empirischen Socialforschung*, Cologne: 1959.

*My then junior coauthors have in their own way remained in the field. Hazel Gaudet is poll editor of the *Public Opinion Quarterly* and Bernard Berelson is president of the Population Council.

Preface to the Second Edition

During the recent war, social scientists had an unprecedented opportunity to contribute their skills and knowledge. Sociologists were called on to study soldier morale, so that the Army could modify attitudes and situations which limited the effectiveness of its operations. Social psychologists were asked to examine propaganda reaching the American public so that that emanating from agencies in our government could be improved, and that disseminated by the enemy counteracted. Anthropologists drew on their knowledge of diverse cultures to advise military governors in ways of avoiding or minimizing frictions in dealing with the Japanese, or the Solomon Islanders, or the Koreans. Economists constantly studied price and production trends in order to determine what price controls and tax policies were necessary.

The success of these researches and the recommendations in which they resulted has enhanced the prestige of the social sciences. More and more frequently government administrators, industry, and labor turn to the social scientist for advice. Postwar events have indeed sharpened this trend. The atom bomb has made us realize how far discoveries in the physical sciences have outrun our ability to integrate them into our social system. The possibility of a third world war, despite universal desires for peace, has made many people wonder to what extent social events are within the control of the various individuals who make up society. In domestic affairs we face problems which seem to require for their solution collective action rather than the free play of competitive forces. Housing and labor relations are only two of the more conspicuous examples. Here again, it is now quite generally accepted that the social sciences can and should make their contribution.

These great expectations place an increased responsibility upon social scientists. If their work is to yield useful and usable knowledge, they must focus their attention on areas of central significance, and they must, at the same time, approach their problems through techniques which lead to empirical facts.

Such requirements mean that three general research problems must be considered. The first relates to the integration of facts and theories. A proper integration of factual materials and theoretical formulations is basic to the existence and development of any science. No one can make use of a mass of unrelated facts; but, conversely, no social action can be based on general speculations about the "nature" of society, if such theories cannot be systematically tested in concrete situations.

Just as empirical research and social theory must be integrated, so actual research findings must also be related to each other. Until recently the social sciences exhibited an unfortunate tendency to conduct a survey here and an experiment there, and to let it go at that. Ph.D. candidates, for example, prided themselves on not repeating a study "which had already been done." Actually, the opposite trend should prevail. Results should be checked and rechecked under both identical and varying conditions. The complexity of social life requires that the same problems be studied many times before basic uniformities can be differentiated from transitory social occurrences.

In the third place the kinds of problems to be studied require careful delineation. In the early history of sociology there were many grandiose schemes for understanding the whole history of mankind. Even at the beginning of this century, when social scientists became more modest, there was still a feeling that "the causes of war" and "methods of preventing crime" could be discovered quickly and easily. Attempts to solve such vast and complex problems soon met opposition.

Causes and changes should not be investigated, it was asserted; social phenomena should merely be described. This position led to a predilection for static, census-like studies which "surveyed" the field but which did not yield findings which could be transferred to social actions.

The way out of this dilemma seems to lie in a compromise, perhaps only temporary. A disciplined and limited kind of dynamic research, focused on social events and developments lasting several months or, at most, several years, appears at the present time to hold most promise. Systematic analyses of political campaigns, of crisis situations, of the development of new communities, of the reactions of different ethnic groups coming into close contact for the first time are most likely to produce the kinds of information on which the future developments of the social sciences depend.

In this Foreword to the second edition of *The People's Choice,* an edition made possible by the Columbia University Press, we shall elaborate these three points. We hope thereby to accomplish two things. First of all, we hope to clarify the major trends in contemporary social research. But we also believe that the reader will find the present study more useful if he reads it with these general developments in mind.

Our discussion of these points will refer to data and observations which either were not included in the original report, or which have been collected in more recent studies.

Let us take up each of these points in reverse order, considering first the need for a type of social research which can study social changes: their origin, nature, and duration.

Dynamic Social Research

Public opinion research is frequently misunderstood at the present time. From poll findings published in magazines and newspapers, laymen, and even colleagues in other social science fields, have gained the impression that such research is content to describe how people feel about a given issue at a particular time. Actually, the scope of this new discipline is much broader

Social scientists want to know the processes by which the various sectors of public opinion influence legislative action and other decision-making in government. Furthermore, we are eager to discover in what ways attitudes themselves are formed. *The People's Choice* focused its attention on this latter problem, the formation, change and development of public opinion.

A group of social scientists remained in Erie County, Ohio, from May until November, 1940, in order to observe the progress and effect of the presidential campaign in that community. A large number of people were interviewed, but the study centered around a panel of 600 respondents who were questioned every month for a period of seven months.

The panel subjects fell into two main groups: those who did not change their political opinion during the period of the study and those who changed in any of a variety of ways. Some shifted their party allegiance, others could not make a decision until the end of the campaign, and still others claimed a definite vote intention but did not go to the polls. These various types of changers and shifters were the central interest of the study, for they were the people in whom the processes of attitude formation and change could be observed. They were compared with the "constant" people. Their personal characteristics, their contacts with other people, and their exposure to radio and newspapers were carefully examined. The reasons they gave for their changes were related to their objective social-economic positions. The opinions they had at one time were contrasted with what they stated at both previous and subsequent interviews. In other words, we did not describe opinion; we studied it *in the making*.

Now let us consider one phase of this dynamic analysis in order to discover its essential elements. The panel was interviewed for the sixth time during October and for the seventh and final time immediately after the election. Thus we know how these people intended to vote shortly before the election and for whom they actually voted. The results are as follows:

			VOTE INTENTION IN OCTOBER		
				Don't	
			Don't	Expect	
Actual Vote	Rep.	Dem.	Know	to Vote	Total
Republican	215	7	4	6	232
Democrat	4	144	12	0	160
Didn't vote	10	16	6	59	91
Total persons	229	167	22	65	483

This simple table has a surprising number of implications. Let us assume for a moment that the interviews in October and November had been conducted with different people, rather than with the same people, as was actually the case. Then, the findings would have read as follows: in October 42 percent (167 out of 396) of those who had a vote intention meant to vote for the Democratic Party; in November 41 percent (160 out of 392) voted for it. This would have given the impression of great constancy in political attitudes. Actually, however, only the people in the major diagonal of the table remained unchanged: 418 out of 483 respondents did what they intended to do; 13 percent changed their minds one way or another.

This 13 percent represents the *turnover* which took place in the few weeks before the election. The concept of turnover is basic for analysis of opinion formation. If the turnover is large, it indicates that the opinion or behavior is unstable. We know that people feel uncertain and that propaganda may be effective, or that clarification and education are required.

If such dynamic research is conducted more frequently in the future, it may be possible to classify social events according to the following dimensions: What types of events show a small or large turnover as they develop? Does the turnover tend to become smaller as the events run their course? At what point is a minimum turnover reached and what is likely to increase it again? Under what conditions do we have a balanced turnover, as in this case, where the changes in various directions seem to cancel each other? When does turnover occur with a shift in "marginal distributions"?

Answers to such questions, however, would give only a rough picture of different social events. We can be more precise. Turnover is the result of changes which come about in the intentions, expectations and behavior of individual persons. Three broad questions can be raised in this connection:

(a) What kind of people are likely to shift?
(b) Under what influences do these shifts come about?
(c) In what directions are the shifts made?

Question (a) can be answered in a variety of ways. Let us concentrate here on the "crystallizers," those people who had no definite vote intention in October but who went to the polls in November. Long before they had reached a decision we could predict rather successfully what they would do: They would decide finally to vote in the same way as did people with similar social characteristics who had made up their minds earlier in the campaign. For example, it is a familiar fact of contemporary American politics, corroborated in this study, that urban people are more likely than rural people to vote for the Democratic Party, and Catholics vote Democratic more frequently than Protestants. If we predict, therefore, that urban, Catholic "Don't knows" will vote for the Democratic Party, we shall be correct in a considerable number of cases, and post-election interviews will verify our predictions.

Such "external correlations" sometimes evoke expressions of disappointment. Turnover analysis, however, permits us to go "inside the situation." We can pick out a variety of psychological mediators which connect the social situation and the individual decision. In each interview, for example, respondents were asked who, in their opinion, would win the election. Even among those who had not yet formed a vote intention, there were many individuals with a definite expectation. And, significantly enough, the expectations expressed by the undecided were not haphazard ones, but instead were usually those prevailing in their own social environments. Following the process one step further, it turned out that expectations foreshadowed final decision: many people voted for the candidate they had previously picked as the winner. Thus these expectations were one of the "intervening" variables which helped in explaining the development of vote decisions. (The details of this analysis are discussed in Chapter XII.)

The table on page xi also suggests answers to questions about the specific influences which produce changes in attitudes or behavior. Again let us focus our attention on one group, those who said in October that they did not intend to vote. It will be noted that the large majority of this group fitted their actions to their words: 59 of the 65 actually did not vote in November. But the six changers, those who shifted from an intention of inaction to an actual vote, all cast their ballots for the Republican candidates. The influences which produced this change were not hard to discover. The field staff in Erie County had observed that, in this election at least, the Republican machine was much more active and efficient than the Democratic. And, indeed, when the six changers were asked what had made them go to the polls, all stated that they had been visited at the last moment by a Republican party worker who had persuaded them to vote.

Thus, by studying the different groups which contribute to the turnover, we can analyze the influences which operate to bring about changes in behavior. This, in itself, provides a large field for investigation. We can record what people read and listen to, and relate such exposure in a twofold way to changes in mind. Some people were aware that they had been influenced by a specific reading or listening experience, and they told us so in the special interviews conducted with all changers. In other cases, a more intricate statistical analysis was necessary to trace the more unconscious influences. (These techniques have been more elaborately discussed in a recent publication.) [1]

In the present study, face-to-face contacts turned out to be the most important influences stimulating opinion change. To

[1] Hans Zeisel, *Say It with Figures* (New York, Harper and Bros., 1947), Chapter X.

the worker in a political machine this is probably not surprising, but to the social scientist it is a challenge. The discovery of the conditions under which attitudes or modes of behavior are particularly accessible to personal influence, the classification of types of personal influence most effective in modifying opinion, the examination of situations in which the more formal influences of mass media seem to produce change, all these are typical problems for what we have called dynamic social research.

But the picture is not completed by knowledge only of who changes and in response to what influences. We also want to know the directions of the changes: Do they result in a random redistribution of opinion, or is there some discernible pattern? Turnover analysis in the present study provided preliminary, but revealing, answers to this question. For particular subgroups within the community, attitude change led to greater uniformity and *homogeneity:* individual changes brought members of specific subgroups into closer agreement with each other. For the community as a whole, however, attitude change produced greater diversity and *polarization:* individual changes brought the members of one subgroup into sharper disagreement with members of other subgroups. We shall consider this process in greater detail in a later section of the foreword. The point to emphasize here is that, through the kind of dynamic research employed in the present study, problems such as the development of group cleavages or increasing awareness of class interests become amenable to social research.

Social Research as a Continuing Endeavor

We are frequently warned that the results of a specific study are valid only for the time and place where it was conducted. Does this mean that the findings of one study can never be duplicated in another? Should we expect different results, even under similar conditions? Questions of this kind suggest that terms such as "repetition" and "corroboration of evidence" need to be considered more carefully. In fact, when similar studies are available, comparative analyses can serve three positive functions:

1. The comparison may indicate that the findings of both studies are the same. This we shall call "the function of *corroboration*."

2. The comparison may indicate that, although the statistical results of the two studies differ, consideration of the specific conditions under which the results were obtained will lead to the same general conclusions. This we shall call "the function of *specification*."

3. A negative result in the first study may be clarified by new findings in the second one. This we shall call "the function of *clarification*."

It happens that the present study can be compared with a similar one. A second but briefer panel study was conducted during the 1944 presidential campaign, four years after the one dealt with in this volume. The Bureau of Applied Social Research, in cooperation with the National Opinion Research Center, then at the University of Denver, conducted two interviews with a nation-wide cross-section of about 2,000 people: one interview before the election, the other after. What will a comparison of these two studies yield? We shall select several examples to illustrate and clarify the functions of comparative analyses.

A first example deals with the corroboration of findings. In the Erie County study, there were 54 party changers, persons who shifted their allegiance from one party to the other. Here again the question about the direction of attitude change arose. Did these party shifts bring the changers in closer harmony with other members of the subgroups to which they belonged, or did the changes occur in some other direction?

In order to answer this we made use of the fact already referred to, namely, that the poor, the urban residents, and the Catholics are more likely to vote the Democratic ticket, while the well-to-do, the Protestants, and the rural dwellers are more frequently found in the Republican camp. On the basis of these three social characteristics, indications of membership in different social groups, it was possible to construct an "index of political predisposition." The index, in turn, permitted us to classify the social backgrounds of all individuals as conducive to either a Democratic or a Republican vote. (For more detailed discussion of the index and the types of analysis which it engendered, see Chapter III in the present study.) It was thus possible to distinguish between two types of individuals: those whose vote intentions were in harmony with their social backgrounds, and the deviate cases whose intentions were at variance with those of the subgroups to which they belonged.

When the 54 party changers were studied, it was found that, before their shifts in party allegiance, 36 individuals had expressed intentions at variance with their social environments, while, after their shifts, only 20 were deviate cases. We thus came to the conclusion that party changes are in the direction of greater consistency and homogeneity within subgroups (p. 139, below).

Because the 1944 study covered only the final few weeks of the campaign, when party changes are rare, it found an even smaller number of shifters. Moreover, an index of political predisposition is less valid when applied to a nation-wide sample than when applied to the residents of one county. And yet, despite these limitations, the results of the second study are an almost *a fortiori* corroboration of those in the first. In 1944 it was possible to study 36 changers. Before their shifts, 22 expressed intentions which deviated from the prevailing opinion climate of their social environments; after the shifts, only 14 deviated.

A comparison of similar studies can thus increase our confidence in findings which might be considered doubtful if only one of the studies had been carried out. Without such corroboration, a finding based on 54 cases in one study and on 36 in a second would be so unreliable that we would question its validity. With the corroboration made possible by successive studies, we are more inclined to accept the result.

Comparative analyses can also confirm general conclusions by indicating that statistically different results are the outcome of different specific conditions. In order to illustrate this function of "specification" we shall return once more to a group of changers already considered: those who said in their pre-election interviews that they would not vote, but who finally went to the polls. In the Erie County study all such individuals voted Republican, while in the 1944 study a majority of these changers voted Democratic. At first glance this might appear to be a contradiction of findings. But is it? In 1940 the Erie County Republican machine was by far the stronger; in 1944 the Political Action Committee was active throughout the nation. Furthermore, P.A.C. concentrated on getting low-income people to the polls on the assumption that, if they voted at all, they would vote Democratic. The figures of the 1944 study prove that assumption correct. Of 20 people (largely from low-income groups) who did not intend to vote but who finally did, 3 cast a Republican and 17 a Democratic ballot.

Thus comparative analyses of studies carried out under different historical or social conditions can lead to much the same sort of confirmation as does actual duplication of results. A comparison of the final decisions of last-minute voters in an election where the Republican machine is strong, with the similar decisions made by similar voters in an election where pro-Democratic forces are active leads to one general conclusion: the machine which makes a strong last-minute effort to get stragglers to the polls can be of great assistance to its party.

Finally, a comparison of similar studies can lead to the clarification of results. In the 1940 study there was some indication that the party changers were the more indifferent voters. This finding was an unexpected one, for political experts have frequently asserted that, during a campaign, the more intelligent and concerned voter will shift his allegiance from one candidate to another as he learns more about their platforms and as he is better able to appraise their qualifications to deal with the foreign and domestic situations which arise. Because the relationship between party changers and indifference was unanticipated, the plan of the 1940 study did not make adequate provisions for examining it.

This was corrected in the 1944 study. Then all respondents who expressed a vote intention in their preelection interviews were asked two questions: Were they much concerned whether or not their candidate won? and, Did they believe there were any important differences between the two candidates? Analysis of the answers to these questions revealed, in fact, that the party changers (those who voted for one candidate after having said they intended to vote for the other) were considerably *less* concerned with the election than were the "constant" voters (those who actually voted as they had previously intended to): 38 percent of the changers, as contrasted with 21 percent of the constant voters, said it made little difference which candidate won the election; 65 percent of the changers, as contrasted with 46 percent of the constant voters, could see no real differences between the candidates. It is important to recognize that these expressions of indifference are not post-factum rationalizations of party changes; they were obtained *before* the change took place.

We can thus clarify a result in the earlier study. The people who change their political opinion are not greatly concerned about the campaign or its outcome. Their indifference makes it difficult for them to reach a lasting decision, for they are easily swayed by fortuitous influences. A conversation with a friend today sways them toward one candidate; a persuasive radio talk yesterday had convinced them to vote for the other party. It is not impossible, in fact, that some of the indifferent voters have not reached a real vote decision even as they enter the polling booths.

We were able to compare only two studies and these only at several points. Yet the comparative analysis was productive. It did increase our confidence in results of the individual studies, and it did confirm some of the broader interpretations. Clearly, then, social scientists have missed a valuable opportunity for adding to the fund of basic knowledge by failing to repeat the same type of study under constant and varying conditions. Panel studies lend themselves particularly well to such repetition: their logic is clear, and comparable aspects of different situations can easily be isolated and contrasted.

Our discussion thus far has indicated research methods and plans through which sociologically relevant and scientifically precise data can be obtained. But social research does not stop with the collection of such information. What is needed further is a systematic integration of the data in a theoretical context. Only then can we expect that the data will, on the one hand, be applicable in concrete social situations, and will, on the other hand, point out the directions in which future research work should move.

Throughout the first edition of *The People's Choice*, we tried to indicate the broader implications of our concrete findings. Further research on specific problems growing out of the original study is now in progress, but much work remains to be done. It should be useful, therefore, to develop more explicitly the theoretical framework in which the study was carried out, and the theoretical implications of its results.

Empirical Data and Social Processes

The Erie County study resulted in a number of generalizations which should be relevant to any research concerned with short-range changes in attitude or behavior. These do not yet form a coherent system. They are generalizations which form a bridge between the facts as they are observed and a more systematic theory which still awaits development. They are statements about social processes, and are, thus, high-order generalizations when contrasted with statements of empirical fact, low-order generalizations when contrasted with the theoretical formulations toward which social research aims.

All of our conclusions about the social processes through

which attitude changes occur are closely interrelated, but for our present purposes it will be sufficient to discuss them separately.

1. A first point concerns the stability of attitudes. The subjects in our study tended to vote as they always had, in fact, as their families always had. Fully 77 percent of the panel members said that their parents and grandparents had voted consistently for one or the other of the major political parties, and they maintained these family traditions in the 1940 election. This stability was made possible by a sort of protective screen built around central attitudes. Despite the flood of propaganda and counterpropaganda available to the prospective voter, he is reached by very little of it. And, when we examine what exactly does reach him, we find that he elects to expose himself to the propaganda with which he already agrees, and to seal himself off from the propaganda with which he might disagree.

2. Such stability cannot be explained by reference to the "stubbornness" or "inertia" of human nature. Whatever other social or psychological functions may be served by the preservation of basic attitudes, it provides a source of great satisfaction to individuals in their group contacts. By maintaining their attitudes intact, they are able to avoid or to minimize conflicts and disagreements with the persons in their social environments who share these attitudes. Thus attitude stability is instrumental in preserving feelings of individual security.

3. These individual tendencies are supplemented by group processes. While the individual preserves his security by sealing himself off from propaganda which threatens his attitudes, he finds those attitudes reinforced in his contacts with other members of his group. Because of their common group membership, they will share similar attitudes and will exhibit similar selective tendencies. But this does not mean that all of the members of a group will expose themselves to exactly the same bits of propaganda or that they will be influenced by precisely the same aspects of common experiences. Each individual will

have his private fund of information and his private catalogue of experiences, even though these are selected and judged according to common standards.

In their mutual interactions, each individual makes public some of the private information and a few of the private experiences which support common attitudes. Thus all individuals become subject to a broader range of selected influences. The interactions serve to increase the isolation of any one individual; they provide him with additional arguments to support his position. The end result of such interactions among group members, then, is a reinforcement, a mutual strengthening, of common attitudes.

4. And yet, change does come about in some cases. It is important, therefore, to determine the conditions under which attitudes lose their stability, and the processes through which the change takes place.

One process depends on the activation of previous experiences and ideas. Every individual carries around with him germs of observations and half-forgotten experiences which are in a sense "recessive," usually because they do not fit into the prevailing traditions or interests of the group to which he belongs. Under certain circumstances, however, during a crisis or during a period of intensive propaganda, these can be brought to the fore. They can then lead to a restructuring of attitudes, and, perhaps in some cases, to a change in group affiliations.

5. Such predispositions to change are more typical for individuals in whom cross-pressures operate. In our complex society, individuals do not belong to one group, only. They have a variety of major social affiliations: their social class, their ethnic group, their religious group, the informal associations in which they participate. These various affiliations will make conflicting claims on some individuals: an upper-class Catholic, for example, may find that his religious affiliation pulls him in one direction, while his class position pulls him in the opposite direction. And when concrete situations, such as

an election campaign, require him to make a definite decision, he must also decide which of his group loyalties should take priority.

The problem of determining how these cross-pressures are resolved is one of the main tasks for social research. The following questions are relevant in this connection: In which of his various group affiliations does the individual experience such conflicting claims? Are there any general rules for predicting which claims will prove the stronger, when several are in conflict? The reader will find that many of the specific findings in the present study are pertinent to this problem, although no safe generalizations about so complex a topic can be made on the basis of a single investigation. The method developed in the Erie County study, however, should provide the means for answering the question. What kind of behavior does an individual under such cross-pressures exhibit? We found in the present study that, compared with the rest of the Erie County population, individuals who experienced cross-pressures took considerably longer to arrive at a definite vote decision. But such delay is not the only possible reaction. Other alternatives range all the way from individual neurotic reactions, such as an inability to make any decisions at all, to intellectual solutions which might lead to new social movements. Many of the baffling questions about the relationship between individual attitudes and social environment may be answered when these problems of cross-pressures and reactions to them are thoroughly and properly studied.

6. But when we talk about an individual and his environment we oversimplify the problem, for the environment consists of other individuals. How are their attitudes developed? Or, to put it somewhat differently, through what mechanisms and processes does a group develop common attitudes?

Again the problem leads us in several directions. We are led, first of all, to study opinion leaders. In every social group there are some individuals who are particularly active and articulate. They are more sensitive than others to the interests of their group, and more anxious to express themselves on important issues. It is relatively easy to locate these individuals, and thus to study how they differ from the majority of their group.

In the present study we found that one of the functions of opinion leaders is to mediate between the mass media and other people in their groups. It is commonly assumed that individuals obtain their information directly from newspapers, radio, and other media. Our findings, however, did not bear this out. The majority of people acquired much of their information and many of their ideas through personal contacts with the opinion leaders in their groups. These latter individuals, in turn, exposed themselves relatively more than others to the mass media. The two-step flow of information is of obvious practical importance for any study of propaganda.

The concept of opinion leadership is, incidentally, not a new one. In the many studies of "power," "influence," and "leadership," we are reminded that every community can point to important men and women who set the fashions and are imitated by others. But our investigation suggests that this familiar concept must be modified. For we found that opinion leadership does not operate only vertically, from top to bottom, but also horizontally: there are opinion leaders in every walk of life.

7. Opinion leadership, however, is only one of the mechanisms through which the attitudes of a group are formed. Another is what has been called the "emergence" or "crystallization" of opinion. Social situations, of which a political campaign would be one example, constantly demand actions or opinions. And the members of a group meet these demands, even when there is no particularly articulate individual on whom they can rely for advice. For, above and beyond opinion leadership are the mutual interactions of group members which reinforce the vague feelings of each individual. As these interactions take place, a new distribution of articulate opinions and attitudes is crystallized.

In essence, then, the process of emergence is another phase of the process of reinforcement discussed above in point (3). When prior attitudes exist, mutual interactions will reinforce them; when no prior attitudes but only vague feelings exist, mutual interactions will crystallize these feelings into definite opinions.

Such emergences of attitude or action have usually been studied only in panic situations, or in attempts to understand "mob behavior." The same processes are at work in many other situations, however, and they do not always lead to turbulence or violence. They occur whenever a stream of propaganda inundates a community, when an important event takes place, or if a group decision is to be made. And, because of their generality, it is important to study under what conditions and in what way these emergences develop.

It is interesting to note that, formulated in this way, questions about the formation of opinion are similar to problems with which economists have struggled for many years. For example, they frequently view the stabilization of price levels as a function of the interactions between supply and the demands of a number of individuals. This is logically similar to considering the distribution of opinion in a group a result of the interactions of many individuals. In neither case can the final result be explained by the previous actions or opinions of individuals considered separately. In both cases the final result is a function of interactions which have as their by-product something which had not existed before.

8. There is still another factor in opinion change. Opinions seem to be organized in a hierarchy of stability. In the course of a campaign, the more flexible ones adapt themselves to the more stable levels. Each political party holds a set of tenets which it tries to impress upon voters. At the beginning of a campaign quite a number of people give "Republican" answers to some questions and "Democratic" answers to others. But as the campaign goes on, there is a tendency for the opinion structure of more and more people to become more and more

homogeneous. When the changes are studied, the topics can be ranked according to their degree of flexibility. Vote intention is most stable; attitudes on more specific topics tend to become consistent with party position. Among these topics, in turn, there are some which seem to be dragged along by others. In the 1940 campaign, for instance, opinions on the personalities of the candidates were relatively more stable, and opinions on specific issues, such as the role of the Government in economic affairs, were likely to be adjusted to the evaluation of the men.

These are only some of the processes through which opinions are formed and modified. But they should help to answer a question raised previously, namely, whether shifts in attitudes move in any definite direction. For, whether the process of change involves the resolution of cross-pressures, the influence of opinion leaders or external events, or mutual interactions, the result of change is increased consistency, both within groups and within individuals. As these processes mold and modify opinions, the group members find themselves in closer agreement with each other; there is thus the simultaneous movement toward increased homogeneity within groups and increased polarization between groups which we described earlier. And correlatively, as the individual conforms more closely to his social environment, as he resolves his cross-pressures and finds vague feelings crystallized into definite opinions, many of the inconsistencies in his private set of attitudes will disappear.

Finally, while these generalizations refine the results of the present study, it is important to recognize their preliminary and tentative character. Investigations of other specific situations may lead to new generalizations or may indicate the need to modify those outlined here. One must keep in mind the relation of a specific study and the type of generalization which we consider. They summarize the information thus far collected, but they are not only summaries. They operate also as guides in new researches, for, with them in mind, we know from the start what to look for. Such generalizations, however, are always too general. The concepts which they imply must be translated into specific indices adapted to the concrete situation. It is through new researches and a constant interplay between data and generalizations that systematic progress is achieved.

Avenues of Further Research

There are four major questions which require further investigation and clarification.

First of all we should like to repeat the present study under different political conditions. Are vote decisions arrived at through different processes when the election centers around important issues? In recent presidential campaigns, such as those studied in 1940 and 1944, there have been few issues on which the major parties were split. As a result, party tradition and machine politics have been potent factors in vote decisions. But there is growing evidence that the Republican and Democratic parties are now moving toward sharper conflict on such basic issues as labor legislation. Future presidential campaigns, then, should provide an opportunity to study how attitudes toward specific issues are crystallized, and how these attitudes are related to vote traditions and group influences.

Much the same sort of information can be obtained by conducting similar studies in local elections. We know that in most of these attention is focused on local issues and that in many of them temporary combinations of interested groups cut across party lines. Under such conditions, party activities are reduced. Before the individual can reach a vote decision, he must make up his mind about specific issues and policies. He may therefore be open to persuasion from various sources, and the processes through which he develops a vote decision may be different from those which operated in recent presidential campaigns.

Secondly, we should like to learn more about the personalities and social backgrounds of individuals who change their attitudes. This would require detailed case studies of both "shifters" and "constants." In the Erie County study, special interviews were conducted with the changers, but limitations of funds did not permit us to go as far as we would have liked or as is necessary.

A third problem concerns the relation of the influences uncovered through panel analysis to the total flow of influences and decision within the community. Panel results can often be understood only when the general background of the community is considered. One of the limitations of the present study, for example, resulted from our failure to study the total community in greater detail. Toward the end of the interviewing we learned from our respondents how important the local Republican machine was in influencing the formation of opinion. By that time, however, it was no longer feasible to study the political situation adequately.

A similar shortcoming was our failure to study the opinion leaders more thoroughly. When the panel subjects mentioned that they had received information or advice from other persons, that fact was recorded and the total incidence of personal influences was determined. But there was no attempt to interview the opinion leaders themselves.

This was remedied in a later research, the results of which will soon appear. Here again the study centered around a panel of respondents, this time in an Illinois community. But here, the opinion leaders received special attention: anyone mentioned by a panel member as being influential was asked a series of special questions designed to determine his sources of information and opinion. In this way we were able to obtain a clearer picture of the flow of influence in that community. We did not view it only through the eyes of individual panel members, but were able to trace it along a series of vertical and horizontal chains.

The fourth challenge is of a methodological nature. Neither the values nor the limitations of panel methods have been fully explored as yet. How long can a panel be retained? On what topics can repeated interviews be used safely, and on what other subjects will repetition bias the information collected in later interviews? Would we gain further insights if we analyzed panel results according to the sophisticated mathematical techniques developed by the time-series analysts? How is current laboratory experimentation on attitude formation related to field studies in which repeated interviews are used?

Fortunately, we have an opportunity to study some of these questions. The Committee on Measurement of Opinion, Attitudes and Consumer Wants, set up by the National Research Council and the Social Science Research Council, obtained funds from the Rockefeller Foundation in order to study the theory and application of panel techniques.

Even during the preliminary phases of the Erie County study it became clear that the technique of repeated interviews was in no way restricted to studies of political propaganda. It is a general method, applicable to any study of attitudes which develop over a period of time. For example, if we want to correct ethnic attitudes, or modify consumer wants, or improve international understanding, we must do more than describe attitudes. We must also study how such attitudes are developed and how they can be influenced. These are all problems for the kind of dynamic social research exemplified in the present study.

Acknowledgments

This study was made financially possible by drawing upon a general grant from the Rockefeller Foundation, the income of the Consulting Division of Columbia University's Office of Radio Research, and by special contributions from *Life* magazine and Elmo Roper.

Mr. Roper was a co-sponsor of the project and he and his staff were most helpful in the planning and execution of the study. Mrs. Carolyn Crucius cooperated in the writing of the questionnaire and in the training of the field staff. Messrs. Robert Williams and Robert Pratt laid out the sample. Mr. Elmo Wilson resided in Sandusky for six months and was in charge of all the work in the field. His resourcefulness in meeting innumerable technical difficulties and the many ideas he contributed to the study as it progressed foreshadowed the important role he was to play later in governmental public opinion research.

Miss Helen Schneider was in charge of the statistical analysis and guided us indefatigably through material which required seven Hollerith punch cards per respondent.

The present report contains only the highlights of an analysis covering several thousand tables and more than a thousand pages of preliminary interpretations. To bring it out in the present form, further help was needed and given.

Mr. M. B. Schnapper, the Executive Secretary of the American Council on Public Affairs, supervised the publication of the manuscript. We are thankful for his expert cooperation.

Dr. Hans Zeisel from McCann-Erickson supervised the production of the charts. He was ably assisted by Ann Hurdman.

Practically every staff member of Columbia University's Office of Radio Research, which is now a Division of its Bureau of Applied Social Research, has at one time or another worked on this study, especially Miss Wyant and Messrs. Farber, Fosberg and Hennig. At several points we had the cooperation of Professor Douglas Waples, Mr. Jesse McKnight, Mr. Alfred Jones, Mr. Fritz Schreir, and Professors Michael Erdelyi, Robert Merton and Goodwin Watson.

The senior author is especially indebted to his colleagues in the Department of Sociology, Columbia University.

PAUL LAZARSFELD
BERNARD BERELSON
HAZEL GAUDET

Bureau of Applied Social Research
Columbia University
Summer, 1944

Contents

CHAPTER I

Introduction

This is a report on modern American political behavior—specifically on the formation of votes during a presidential campaign. Every four years, the country stages a large-scale experiment in political propaganda and public opinion. The stimuli are comprised of everything the two parties do to elect their candidates. What the people do in the course of this campaign represents the reactions reviewed and analyzed in these pages.

We are interested here in all those conditions which determine the political behavior of people. Briefly, our problem is this: to discover how and why people decided to vote as they did. What were the major influences upon them during the campaign of 1940? We believe we know some of the answers; we are sure we do not know them all. Similar studies of a series of major elections, especially in comparison with one another, will confirm the valid findings of this report, correct its deficiencies, and in general clarify and complete existing knowledge of the determinants of political opinion in a modern democracy.

There are several ways to analyze elections. Until relatively recently, official vote records constituted the only available material on elections. They were useful for the study of the geographical distribution of the political temper of the people and not much else. Then a group of political scientists centering around the University of Chicago introduced what might be called the ecological analysis of voting. By examining vote records for small units of a city or state for which a considerable number of background (census) data were available, they were able to isolate to some extent the effects upon vote of such factors as religion and nationality and gross economic status. Although they worked under the handicap of dealing with voters in the large—e.g., not everyone living in a predominantly Irish district was an Irishman—nevertheless they increased our understanding of some major determinants of political decision.

Then came the public opinion polls and they advanced our knowledge by relating political opinion to the characteristics of the individual voter and by revealing vote intentions before the election itself. Thus they made much more precise the study of certain determinants of vote and, to some extent, they made possible the study of the development of vote during a political campaign.

But it was at this very point that further progress was needed. The full effect of a campaign cannot be investigated through a sequence of polls conducted with different people. They show only majority tendencies which are actually the residual result of various sorts of changes—to or from indecision and from one party to the other. They conceal minor changes which cancel out one another and even major changes if they are countered by opposing trends. And most of all, they do not show *who* is changing. They do not follow the vagaries of the individual voter along the path to his vote, to discover the relative effect of various influential factors upon his final vote.

In short, never before has the development of the person's vote been traced throughout a political campaign, from his preconvention attitudes through his reactions to the barrage of propaganda which constitutes the campaign proper to his actual vote on Election Day. Only by such an investigation can we establish more closely the roles of the several influences upon vote (and other political attitudes), from both predispositions and stimuli. This study, designed to yield such answers, used the so-called panel technique as the next step forward in opinion research: *repeated interviewing of the same people.*

A New Research Method

Let us briefly examine the technical plan of the investigation; an outline of it is represented by the graphical scheme shown in Chart 1.

The survey was done in Erie County, Ohio, located on Lake Erie between Cleveland and Toledo. This county was chosen because it was small enough to permit close supervision of the interviewers, because it was relatively free from sectional peculiarities, because it was not dominated by any large urban center although it did furnish an opportunity to compare rural political opinion with opinion in a small urban center, and because for forty years—in every presidential election in the twentieth century—it had deviated very little from the national voting trends. Because of the diversity of American life, there is no such thing as a "typical American county." But it is not unlikely that Erie County was as representative of the northern and western sections of the country as any similarly small area could be. In any case, we were studying the *development* of votes and not their distribution.

In May, 1940, every fourth house in Erie County was visited by a member of the staff of from twelve to fifteen specially trained local interviewers, chiefly women. In this way, approximately 3,000 persons were chosen to represent as closely as possible the population of the county as a whole. This group— the poll—resembled the county in age, sex, residence, education, telephone and car ownership, and nativity.

From this poll, four groups of 600 persons each were selected by stratified sampling. Each group was closely matched to the others and constituted, in effect, a miniature sample of the whole poll and of the county itself.[1] Of these four groups of 600, three were reinterviewed only once each—one in July, one in August, and one in October. They were used as "control groups" to test the effect that repeated interviewing might have on the panel.[2] At the same time they provided a larger sample (1,200 respondents) on a variety of important ques-

CHART 1
OUTLINE OF THE STUDY

Time Table	May	June	July	August	September	October	November
			REPUBLICAN CONVENTION	DEMOCRATIC CONVENTION		ELECTION	
Interview Number	1	2	3	4	5	6	7
Group	Total Poll	Main Panel 600	Main Panel 600	Main Panel 600	Main Panel 600	Main Panel 600	Main Panel 600
Interviewed	(3000)		Control A 600	Control B 600		Control C 600	

tions asked at the control points. The fourth group—the panel
—was interviewed once each month from May to November.

Interviews were spaced about a month apart to fit best the
natural course of campaign events. The first two interviews
were made in May and June, prior to the Republican Convention—the original poll and the first recall on the panel members. The third interview came in July, between the two conventions, and the fourth in August, after both conventions. Two
more calls were made between the conventions and Election
Day, the second as close to the eve of the election as possible.
The seventh and last interview was made in November, shortly
after the election.

Thus, the 600 people of the panel were kept under continual
observation from May until November, 1940. Whenever a person changed his vote intention in any way, from one interview
to the next, detailed information was gathered on why he had
changed. The respondents were also interviewed regularly on
their exposure to campaign propaganda in all the media of
communication— the press, radio, personal contacts, and others.
In addition, the repeated interviews made it possible to secure
voluminous information about each respondent's personal characteristics, social philosophy, political history, personality traits,
relationships with other people, opinions on issues related to the
election—in short, information on anything which might contribute to our knowledge of the formation of his political preferences.[3]

Let us demonstrate the yield of the panel technique in the
case of a particular individual. This example is atypical in that
he changed his mind more frequently than the average voter
but he was deliberately selected in order to show how such
changes can be followed through repeated interviewing.

This young man, undecided in May, voted for Roosevelt in
November. But it would be incorrect to assume that at some
point during the campaign he simply made up his mind once
and for all. Actually, he followed a devious route on his way to
the polls. He was a first voter with some high school educa-

tion and with a slightly better than average socio-economic level. At first he favored Taft for the Republican nomination because he was a fellow resident of Ohio, but on the other side of his indecision was his tendency to vote Democratic "because my grandfather is affiliated with that party." This tendency won out in July when he announced that he would vote for Roosevelt to please his grandfather. In August, however, his opposition to the President's stand on conscription gained the upper hand and he came out for Willkie, even though he knew little about him. At this point his vote intention represented a vote against conscription and Roosevelt's pressure for it. At the same time, he generalized this disapproval of conscription into a disapproval of the third term. The following month he changed again: he simply did not know enough about Willkie to cling to him so he reverted to a state of indecision and began to think that he would not vote at all. This attitude persisted throughout the last days of the campaign, when he indicated that the outcome of the election did not make any difference to him. During August and September he believed Willkie would win but later he was undecided on that too, partly because a movie audience had booed the Republican candidate in a news-reel appearance a few days before. But on Election Day, he voted for Roosevelt. He was repelled at the very end of the campaign by what he considered Willkie's begging for votes and he was strongly influenced by fellow workers at the foundry where he was employed. The saga of the formation of his vote illustrates the kinds of data not available before the develop-ment of the repeated interview technique.

In summary, then, the panel was devised as a more effective method of getting at the important questions. What is the effect of social status upon vote? How are people influenced by the party conventions and the nominations? What role does formal propaganda play? How about the press and the radio? What of the influence of family and friends? Where do issues come in, and how? Why do some people settle their vote early and some late? In short, how do votes develop? Why do people vote as they do? By inference and by direct accounts of the respondents, we shall try to show what influences operated between May and November to determine the ballots cast on November 5, 1940.

Before pushing on to the findings themselves, let us summarize briefly the major contributions of the panel technique.

(1) We can determine who the changers are during the campaign and can study their characteristics. The best example of this kind of analysis will be found in Chapters VI and VII.

(2) We can accumulate information pertaining to the whole campaign from one interview to the next. For example, we are able to distinguish people according to whether they were exposed to predominantly Republican or predominantly Democratic propaganda, on the basis of indices constructed from their answers at different times. Examples appear in Chapters V, X, and XIV.

(3) When a respondent changes his vote intention between two interviews, we catch his opinion in a process of flux. It obviously tells us little to ask a man who has voted Republican all his life why he favors the present Republican candidate. If, however, a respondent intended to vote Democratic last month and this month intends to vote Republican, the reasons for his change enable us to gauge the effectiveness of the propaganda and other influences to which he was subjected. Such information is discussed, for example, in Chapters IV, VIII, IX, and X.

(4) Repeated interviews also permit us to trace the effects of propaganda statistically. For example, we can study the people who are undecided at one interview but who have an opinion at the next. Anything such people did or thought at the time of the first interview, then, precedes the time of their decision. By studying such data, we can infer what made the respondents decide as they did. This kind of information is quite different from that found in the usual public opinion surveys, which provide data related to opinion at the same point in time. There we cannot tell what is cause and what is effect, but the repeated interview technique allows us to establish a time se-

quence and therefore greatly facilitates causal analysis. Examples of this sort of analysis will be found in Chapters VIII, XII, and XV.

A Guide for the Reader

Finally, a brief preview of the organization of the book may serve as orientation. The following chapter, describing the county in which this study was made and recalling the time of the study, completes the introduction. The next three chapters, on the social and ideological differences between the parties and on the voters' degree of participation in the election, deal with the more or less stable characteristics of the respondents. These early chapters serve a twofold purpose: they report findings important in their own right and they set the background against which much of the rest of the study must be seen.

Once we have established the basic differences between the supporters of the two major parties, we move on in Chapters VI and VII to characterize the changers—the people who changed their vote intention in one way or another during the campaign proper. Such people are of particular interest because they are the only ones who decide how to vote while the campaign is going on. First the characteristics of three types of voters are compared: those who decide how to vote before the campaign starts, those who decide during the convention period, and those who do not decide until late in the campaign. We then turn to a consideration of the different kinds of vote changers, i.e., the different ways in which people whose vote intention fluctuates one way or another finally come to a definite vote decision.

Then follows a section of four chapters (Chapters VIII to XI) dealing with the effects of the campaign upon the various groups of voters previously delineated. Each of the three major effects of the campaign is discussed in a separate chapter, and their comparative importance is considered in Chapter XI.

This four-chapter section discusses the effects of the campaign as a whole. The final chapters deal with the role of several specific campaign influences. Chapter XII indicates the role of expectations—speculations about the winner, the bandwagon effect, etc. Chapter XIII reveals the nature of the political content of the newspapers, magazines, and radio programs to which the respondents were exposed during the campaign and then Chapter XIV takes up the role of these formal media of communication in bringing people to their vote decisions. Chapter XV considers the role of social groups in maximizing political agreement among their members and Chapter XVI relates this political homogeneity to the effect of person-to-person contacts.

In short, this report progresses from the background characteristics of the electorate to an analysis of the people who change their minds during the campaign, to a presentation of the influences of the campaign as a whole, and finally to a discussion of the sources of such influence.

CHAPTER II

Erie County, Ohio, 1940

A brief outline of the locale and of the background events will serve to orient the study as a whole.

Erie County in 1940 was small, reasonably prosperous, peopled with a homogeneous, friendly group of native Americans engaged about equally in agricultural and industrial work. As mentioned in the preceding chapter, it was not the "typical American county" but for the purposes of this study it did not need to be. We were not interested in *how* people voted but in *why* they voted as they did. We did not want to predict the outcome of the election but to discover certain processes underlying opinion formation and political behavior.

The county was a prosperous-looking area of gently rolling terrain, fronting on Lake Erie in the north-central portion of Ohio. Located on a good harbor, almost midway between Cleveland and Toledo, the county had excellent transportation facilities by road, by rail, and by water.

Relatively stable for forty years, the population of Erie County in 1940 was 43,000. The county seat of Sandusky, the only urban industrial community in the county, had a population of approximately 25,000. The people living in the county were almost all native-born white. About a quarter of the inhabitants were descendants mainly of Germans who settled there sometime in the middle of the nineteenth century. The people were largely of the working class, with a sprinkling of upper-class merchants, manufacturers, and professional men. There were few families of wealth and they did not dominate the area. There were lower-class families but, with the exception of the few Negro families in Sandusky, they were not located in clusters. There were few spots which might be designated as slums in the town and there were no rural slums.

The cultural and social life of the county was perhaps not atypical of the middle-western small-town and rural section. The people depended on simple things for pleasures. The family was an important social unit (and political as well, as we shall see later), with considerable social activity going on in the home. Sandusky was known as a "church town" and the church was often the core of social life. Each church had a wide range of organizations for men, women and children. The preachers were conservative: they preached the gospel and did not participate much in civic or political affairs. Fraternal and business groups were normally active as were the usual forum and discussion groups. The school system was manned by competent, progressive, non-partisan elements. The Catholic Church maintained a few parochial schools, but the attendance in the public schools was about ten times as large. There was no college in the county but education in the formal sense appeared to receive the support of the population at large and the teaching profession was respected within the community. The educational level of the county was considerably above the average for the United States as a whole. By and large, the people in Erie County gave the appearance of mingling without any great degree of "class consciousness."

There were three local newspapers in Sandusky—few towns of that size have so many—and in addition to them the people of the county read the *Cleveland Plain Dealer* and a smattering of other out-of-town papers. Of the local papers, one was strongly Republican, one nominally Democratic but actually neutral, and one mildly and belatedly Democratic. The *Cleveland Plain Dealer* broke with its Democratic tradition in 1940 and came out for Willkie. Cleveland and Toledo radio stations covering all the major networks had good reception in Erie County.

The Economy of the County

The economy of Erie County was of a mixed industrial and agricultural type. There was little industry outside of Sandusky; agriculture was the principal pursuit in the rest of the county. The land had been cultivated for many years and crops were usually good, in many instances better than the state average. Compared to the nation as a whole, the farm population was quite prosperous. A few farm organizations devoted themselves mainly to agricultural problems; political matters were seldom touched upon directly.

The industry of the county was perhaps unusual in that it was scattered among 60 establishments employing about 3,000 persons in all and producing a widely diversified array of manufactured items. The largest plant operating in the area at the time was a paper-box concern employing 900 workers. Sandusky, with a good harbor, was an important port on the Great Lakes in tonnage shipped, the chief load being coal.

Due partly to the variety of industrial enterprises and partly to widespread dependence upon agriculture, the county escaped much of the violence of economic shifts during the depression years. The tenor of business affairs was generally conservative and cautious. Most of the plants and enterprises were locally owned and operated with comparatively little outside money invested in the business. With little absentee ownership, the common pattern was that of a closely held, family-unit type of business. In spite of the large number of small businesses in the town, industrial control of the city was well established during the years preceding 1940. There had been some conflict within business circles regarding the advisability of attracting new industry to the community, and the opposition faction was largely successful in blocking expansion and maintaining a labor situation favorable to the employers. Because the supply of labor was plentiful, the prevailing wage rate was low. Local union leadership had not been outstanding or progressive or particularly aggressive and local units were not active in their own state organizations. Labor was not an important influence in the county; the domination of business over labor was freely admitted by local labor leaders. Only Sandusky contained labor organizations and that city was essentially an open-shop community. Labor did not form a political bloc as such, and no group or individual was able to deliver the labor vote. On the whole, the labor picture was apathetic rather than calm.

The County and Politics

There were no special interest groups in Erie County wielding important political influence. None of the ethnic groups— Negroes, Germans, or others—formed an organized voting unit. The minority parties were not strong and there was no youth movement in the county (although there was a Young Republican Club). The votes of neither veteran nor fraternal groups could be delivered; and there were too few relief clients for them to be influential as a unit.

The 1940 campaign found the Republican party organization tightly knit throughout the county and the Democratic organization split and much less effective. Several factors contributed to this state of affairs. First, the Democrats locally and within the state had long been subject to friction within their ranks. Again, the Republicans had more party funds with which to operate. And finally, the Republicans had been out of office so long that they felt keenly the need to organize. Each of the party organizations did a certain amount of face-to-face work but the better-organized Republicans did a more effective job, depending to a large extent on the strength of the women's organizations.

The Setting of the Study

On November 5, 1940, the people of the United States went to the polls to elect a president to lead them through the crucial years of the war. Hitler's blitzkrieg was in full swing. He had already taken over Austria, Poland, and Czechoslovakia, and during the pre-election period his armies marched through the Low Countries and conquered France. Just before the election, his ally Italy invaded Greece. The United States traded some old warships to Britain for naval and air bases in the Atlantic. Military conscription was begun. The wholesale suppression of civil rights in the totalitarian countries highlighted the picture of a nation democratically choosing a leader amid free discussion.

The 1940 campaign also gained interest from the sharply delineated personalities of the major candidates. Each had broken precedents in a spectacular way. One was the incumbent running for a third term; the other had risen meteorically to become the nominee of the party against which he had voted throughout most of his career.

The major events—local, national and international—which occurred during the period of the campaign and of the study are represented in Chart 2. They may help to recall the atmosphere of the 1940 campaign.

CHART 2

1940 Campaign Events in Erie County

Period	Local Events	National Events	International Events
Last half of June	Second interview of panel respondents	Knox and Stimson appointed to cabinet GOP votes peace platform. Willkie and McNary nominated.	France asks for peace French sign Hitler's terms French-Italian armistice signed
First half of July	Third interview of panel, second interview of "Control A"	Mrs. Roosevelt speaks in Lakeside, Ohio Roosevelt says he will not send men overseas.	Churchill announces bulk of French fleet seized or destroyed Laval announces "corporative" state
Second half of July		Roosevelt and Wallace nominated at Democratic Convention	Pan-American Conference in Havana

First half of August	Fourth interview of panel, second interview of "Control B"	Debate on conscription begins Lindbergh urges cooperation with Germany if Axis wins Roosevelt reiterates: no foreign service for U.S. soldiers	
Second half of August	*Cleveland Plain Dealer* switches to Willkie	Willkie makes acceptance speech at Elwood, Ind. Wallace resigns cabinet post Alien registration Senate passes draft bill	British bomb Berlin in first big raid.
First half of September		FDR's Labor Day speech calling upon the U.S. to unite for total defense Congress passes Draft Act	Britain gets U.S. ships in exchange for air and navy bases First of 14 days of London air raids
Second half of September	Fifth interview of panel	Roosevelt signs Draft Act U.S. bans scrap iron sale to Japan Willkie campaign trip through the Middle and Far West (8 major speeches)	German - Italian - Japanese 10-year military alliance
First half of October	Willkie speaks in Sandusky Last day for vote registration	Roosevelt visits Ohio in "non-political" defense inspection trip	Balkan crisis
Last half of October	*Sandusky News* backs Roosevelt Sixth interview of panel, second interview of "Control C" Gerald L. K. Smith addresses 3,000 people in Willkie rally in Sandusky	Conscription registration John L. Lewis backs Willkie Willkie in the Midwest and East (8 major speeches) Roosevelt's first three political speeches of the campaign	Italy invades Greece
First half of November	Seventh interview of panel	Last campaign speeches: Roosevelt in Brooklyn and Cleveland; Willkie in New York Election Day, November 5th	

CHAPTER III

Social Differences between
Republicans and Democrats

Any practical politician worth his salt knows a great deal about the stratification of the American electorate. It is part of his everyday working equipment to know what kinds of people are likely to be dyed-in-the-wool Republicans or traditional Democrats. He would not be in business long if he did not know who was most susceptible to the arguments of either party.

Today, in most sections of the country, the politician can count on the banker, the business manager, the farmer, the bishop and a good many of his flock to vote Republican. In the same way, he knows that the immigrant, the working man, the priest and most of his parishioners—particularly those in cities —constitute the mainstay of the Democratic party outside the Solid South.

The features by which the politician differentiates a Republican and a Democrat, then, seem to be economic status, religion, residence, and occupation. To these can be added a fifth—age. Tradition has it that youth shuns the conservative, in politics as well as in clothes, music, and manners.

For the most part, the study of Erie County's voting behavior in 1940 confirms this voice of experience. But it does more than merely lend scientific status to common-sense knowledge. By systematizing the knowledge, by giving an actual measure of the influence of each of these factors of stratification, the study places them in their proper rank-order and brings out their interdependence.

The Role of Socio-Economic Status

Before discussing the role which socio-economic status plays in the composition of the two major political parties, let us consider the index by which we measure this characteristic.

Public opinion research customarily makes use of interviewers' ratings of socio-economic status. For convenience let us refer to them as SES ratings. Interviewers are trained to assess the homes, possessions, appearance, and manner of speech of the respondents and to classify them into their proper stratum in the community according to a set quota. The people with the best homes, furniture, clothes, etc., i.e., the ones with the most money, would be classed as A's; and the people at the other extreme would be D's. In Erie County, the quota was approximated in the following distribution: A, 3%; B, 14%; C+, 33%; C—, 30%; and D, 20%[1].

There are a number of general considerations implied in such a classification which can only briefly be summarized here.[2] The first question concerns the reliability of such a classification procedure. Would two independent tests yield the same results? We have some evidence on this question. Experiments have shown that two sets of ratings, representing two independent appraisals of the same subjects by the same interviewers but spaced three weeks apart, have a correlation of .8. When the same subjects are observed by two different interviewers, the correlation goes down to .6 or .7.[3] Although there is some variation, then, the ratings provide a fairly stable classification.

But do these ratings classify people so that the result corresponds to general experience? Again there is evidence to show that the SES ratings are closely related to the material possessions of the respondents. The higher the rating, the higher the average income, the average number of expensive household articles owned, and so on.[4]

These SES ratings are closely related to the educational level of the subjects. Also, the higher ratings go to business and professional people, while the lower ones are given mainly to workers and manual laborers.

In short, special studies have shown that these qualitative ratings represent a sort of average of, or common factor to, the various status ratings for the different specific social groups with which people are associated. It is well known, for example, that in many communities a family name that dates from centuries back brings more prestige than does wealth. A respondent with money *and* family status is ranked higher by interviewers than one who qualifies on only one of these two points. And the latter person, in turn, would be placed ahead of someone who had neither money nor a time-honored name. The SES ratings can therefore be considered a measure of the number of qualifications each respondent has for a high rank on the socio-economic scale.[5] In this sense, the SES ratings represent a general stratification index.

Now, to what extent did the SES levels differentiate party vote? To what extent did people on the various levels support the Republicans or the Democrats? The answer is that there were twice as many Republicans on the A level as on the D level (Chart 3). And with each step down the SES scale, the proportion of Republicans decreases and the proportion of Democrats correspondingly increases.

Such a general index, useful as it is in establishing general relationships, often obscures interesting nuances. For example, a sociologist interested in the concept of "class" might believe that such an index of socio-economic stratification befogs the issue more than it clarifies it. He might suggest that it is the objective and concrete position of the individual in the general system of business and production that really matters. For a statistical answer to this problem, a sub-classification of the respondents *within* the different SES levels is necessary. Although it is not the purpose of this study to consider stratification systems in any great detail, an example or two of such sub-classifications will show that the *general* SES index does not obscure the more refined problems of social stratification, but rather aids in the study of them.

As a first basis for further classification (Chart 4), we can

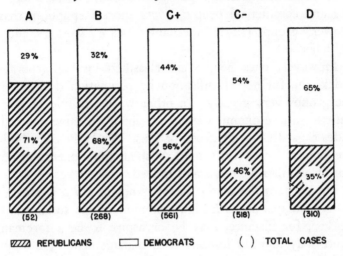

CHART 3[6]

Those high in socio-economic status (SES level) are more likely to vote Republican than Democratic.

REPUBLICANS   DEMOCRATS   ( ) TOTAL CASES

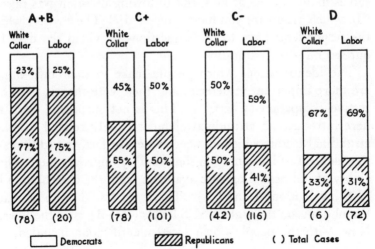

CHART 4

Fewer laborers than white-collar workers vote Republican but if SES level is held constant, occupation makes little difference.

Democrats   Republicans   ( ) Total Cases

use the occupations of our respondents. On each SES level, the "upper" occupational groups—professionals, business men, clerical and commercial people—were more Republican than the "lower" groups (skilled mechanics, factory workers, and manual laborers).[7]

However, once people are classified by the general SES index, the further classification by occupation does not refine the groups very greatly. In other words, people of the same general socio-economic status have about the same political attitudes regardless of their occupations. When the contribution of the general SES level is held constant, the influence of occupation itself upon vote is small indeed.

But perhaps the crucial factor is not so much a person's objective occupation as his own opinion of his social status. A worker, for instance, may be or aspire to be a foreman and hence may identify himself with management. He may then feel that his personal welfare is linked to the welfare of business rather than labor. Perhaps a person's own "class" identification influences his vote more than his actual occupation. In order to study this possibility, the following question was asked in October and November:[8] "To which of the following groups do you feel you belong?" For those who did not consider themselves in any of the groups, the following question was raised: "In which group are you most interested?" The answers which the respondents gave to these questions provided the data for our second sub-classification.

The identifications which people make in their own minds are more important in determining their vote than is their objective occupation (Chart 5). This is not surprising since we here introduce an attitudinal element closely related to other attitudinal factors which influence vote. In fact, the addition of this element of identification considerably improves the predictability of political allegiance available from the classification by SES levels alone (Chart 3). There we found twice as many Republicans on the highest SES levels $(A+B)$ as on the lowest. Now, with the people's own social identification included, the

CHART 5

*Whereas actual occupation does little to refine the relation-
ship between SES level and vote, it makes more difference
whether a voter considers himself as belonging to "business"
or "labor."*

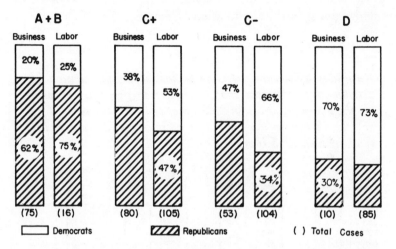

A+B		C+		C-		D	
Business	Labor	Business	Labor	Business	Labor	Business	Labor
20%	25%	38%	53%	47%	66%	70%	73%
62%	75%	47%		34%		30%	
(75)	(16)	(80)	(105)	(53)	(104)	(10)	(85)

☐ Democrats ▨ Republicans ( ) Total Cases

discrimination has increased to a ratio of almost three-to-one.

In short, the general SES index can be refined by combination with other social measures—particularly identification. As
the social characterization of the respondent becomes more detailed a closer relationship to political affiliation can be established. The wealthier people, the people with more and better
possessions, the people with business interests—these people
were usually Republicans. The poorer people, the people whose
homes and clothes were of lower quality, the self-acknowledged
laboring class—they voted Democratic. Different social characteristics, different votes.

Religious Affiliation and Age

In Erie County there was another factor which was no less
important than SES level. That was religious affiliation.
Sixty percent of the Protestants and only 23% of the Catho-

lics had Republican vote intentions in May. At first glance, this might appear to be a spurious result. As a group, Catholics are ordinarily lower in economic status than Protestants and hence this result may simply reflect SES levels. But it does not. On each SES level, religious affiliation plays an important role in determining political affiliation (Chart 6).

CHART 6

Religious affiliation splits vote sharply. This cannot be attributed to the fact that Catholics in this country are, on the average, lower in SES level than Protestants. The relationship between vote and religious affiliation holds true on each SES level.

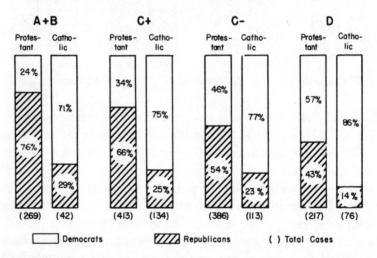

This difference between Protestants and Catholics may have several explanations. Perhaps it was due to differences in the national origins of the religious groups. In the big cities, the Irish, Polish, and Italian people—most of whom are Catholic —have strong ties with the Democratic party. But this is not adequate to explain the voting behavior of Erie County Catholics. For there was only one nationality group, other than the Anglo-Saxon, of any appreciable size in Erie County—the German. The religious composition of this group was the same as that of the rest of the population residing in Erie County.

But that attempt at explanation, unsatisfactory in itself, contains the germ of another hypothesis which undoubtedly has greater validity. The Catholics have traditionally been affiliated with the Democratic party through the waves of Irish, Italian, and Polish immigration. Many Democratic party leaders have been Catholics—note these recent chairmen of the national committee: Raskob, Farley, Flynn, Walker, Hannegan— and Al Smith, the Democratic candidate in 1928, is the only Catholic ever nominated for the Presidency. The political affiliation of the Catholics is explained, to some extent, by this simple historical fact.

It is possible, too, that this tendency is reinforced by the traditional inclination of the Catholic clergy toward the Democratic party developing out of the immigration history of the different European nationalities. Although the priests may not have exerted any direct influence, their preferences probably filtered through to their religious communities. It is not unlikely that some parishioners, especially those not too interested in politics in the first place, simply follow the lead of their priest as an expression of the group solidarity so frequently found among Catholics.

Another possibility is that the predominant Democratic vote of the Catholics is the expression of an out-group supporting the out-party. In most American communities, the Catholics are in the minority when compared with the Protestants as a whole; and in most northern communities the Democrats represent a minority party despite their recent successes, since the "normal" vote is Republican. The Catholics may vote Democratic as an affirmation of this common minority identification.[9]

The differences in the political inclinations of the two religious groups serves to introduce the relationship between age and vote preference. Legend has it that older people are more conservative in most things, including politics, both because they like to perpetuate their own idealized past and because they have more to conserve. By the same token, younger people are more liberal, more receptive to change. If one accepts the common stereotypes—that the Republican party is more "conservative" and the Democrats more "liberal"—then the legend seems to hold for Erie County in 1940.

In May, 50% of those below 45 years of age, but 55% of those over 45 intended to vote Republican. However, this result does not hold for the Protestants and Catholics separately (Chart 7). Only among the Protestants were the older people

CHART 7[10]

Within each religious group the younger voters show tendencies of opposition. Younger Protestants vote less Republican than older Protestants, and younger Catholics less Democratic than older Catholics.

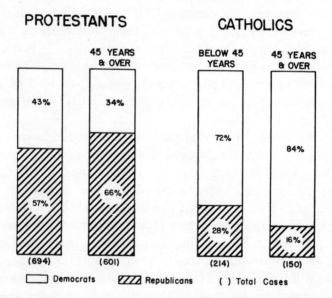

more Republican. Among the Catholics, the relationship was reversed: the older people were more Democratic. This refinement of the relationship between age and political preference probably has two explanations. First, the younger people, who are generally less church-influenced than their elders, show less influence of religion upon vote. Thus young Protestants are less Republican than old Protestants and young Catholics less Democratic than old Catholics. And secondly, the myth that age brings political conservatism—here shown to be incorrect—may apply in another sense. Like appetite, custom grows by what it feeds on. The religious factors which influence vote preference are intensified through the years so that they carry more weight for the elderly. They have a longer time to exercise their influence, to indoctrinate the respondent, to affect him through the common elements. In other words, advancing age may not bring *political* conservatism but it does bring *social* conservatism.

An Index of Political Predisposition

To this point, we have isolated two major influences upon vote: the SES level and religious affiliation. And, incidentally, we have seen that the political effect of age differs for Catholics and Protestants. A number of other factors were investigated, but only one proved statistically significant: there were 14% more Republican voters in the rural part of the county than in Sandusky, the one large industrialized town with a population of 25,000.

Other differences were less important. Women were somewhat more inclined to favor the Republican party. The same was true for better-educated people, but education is so highly related to SES level that it is hard to say whether the influence of education alone would be distinguishable if a more refined economic classification were used.

The multiple correlation between vote and the social factors discussed above is approximately .5.[11] But the greatest part of the predictive value of all these factors derives from three factors: SES level, religion, and residence. Of all rich Protestant farmers almost 75% voted Republican, whereas 90% of the Catholic laborers living in Sandusky voted Democratic.

In order to use these factors in a simple way, we constructed an index of political predisposition (IPP)[12] so that the respondents could be classified on a scale ranging from those with strong Republican predispositions at one extreme to those with strong Democratic predispositions at the other. While an index is, of course, cruder than a coefficient of multiple correlation, it does serve to distinguish easily among the votes of people with different combinations of personal characteristics (Chart 8). The proportion of Republicans falls off consistently and signifi-

CHART 8

High SES level, affiliation with the Protestant religion, and rural residence predispose a voter for the Republican party; the opposites of these factors make for Democratic predisposition. Summarized in an index of political predisposition (IPP), their effect is illustrated by the high correlation with vote intention.

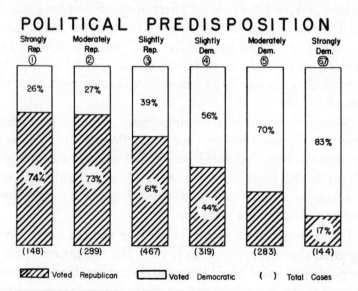

POLITICAL PREDISPOSITION

Strongly Rep. ①	Moderately Rep. ②	Slightly Rep. ③	Slightly Dem. ④	Moderately Dem. ⑤	Strongly Dem. ⑥⑦
26%	27%	39%	56%	70%	83%
74%	73%	61%	44%		17%
(148)	(289)	(467)	(319)	(283)	(144)

▨▨▨ Voted Republican   ☐ Voted Democratic   ( ) Total Cases

cantly from one extreme of political predispositions to the other. And thus a simple combination of three primary personal characteristics goes a long way in "explaining" political preferences.

There is a familiar adage in American folklore to the effect that a person is only what he thinks he is, an adage which reflects the typically American notion of unlimited opportunity, the tendency toward self-betterment, etc. Now we find that the reverse of the adage is true: a person thinks, politically, as he is, socially. Social characteristics determine political preference.

CHAPTER IV

Ideological Differences between Republicans and Democrats

Some of the objective characteristics which distinguished the average Republican voter from his Democratic counterpart have now been described. To what extent did the two groups differ in their thinking about public affairs, especially about the issues involved in the election?

The first question is whether the social stratification of the two parties was reflected in attitudes toward social and economic matters. There is a variety of sources from which we derive an affirmative answer. As a matter of fact, the difference in the social philosophies of the two groups of voters was even more pronounced than their social composition.

Economic and Social Attitudes

The task of propaganda in a political campaign is to arouse expectations among the voters. What they believe the victory of their candidate will mean for the country or for themselves should indicate the social philosophy of the two party groups. We therefore asked our panel the following two questions: "What class of people do you think would benefit most by the election of Roosevelt? What class of people do you think would benefit most by the election of Willkie?"

The picture of the two candidates as seen through the eyes of the voters was fairly similar for Republicans and Democrats. A very large majority of both groups thought that it would be the common man, the plain people, the working class, who would benefit if Roosevelt were elected. Both groups also agreed, although not to the same extent, that Willkie's victory would be best for the business class. But there were a number of finer distinctions which shed light not only on the image of the two candidates but also on the attitude of the electorate itself.

Seventy-six per cent of the Democrats and 64% of the Republicans thought that the common people would benefit most by the re-election of Roosevelt. But three-quarters of the Democrats explicitly used terms of reference such as "workers" or "laborers" while an equally large majority of the Republicans talked about "WPA jobholders," "relief people," or "unemployed." The two groups therefore were agreed on what the social meaning of a Roosevelt victory would be, but his opponents felt that the people whom Roosevelt would try to help were not the most valuable element of the population. In 1940, the connotations of the term unemployment were still traumatic. Forty-one per cent of the Republicans stressed that the unemployed would benefit by a Roosevelt victory, but only 3% of the Democrats used this term. Apparently both groups felt that "unemployed" was a derogatory term. Obviously, unemployment is still not regarded as an economic phenomenon.

The picture of Willkie was somewhat less clearly defined. For one thing there were many more in both party groups who did not know *who* would benefit most from his victory. And the two parties did not agree on Willkie as clearly as they did on Roosevelt. Fifty-seven per cent of the Democrats felt that business groups would benefit most from a Willkie victory, but only 25% of the Republicans thought so. Nineteen per cent of the Republicans claimed that his victory would be beneficial for the working class and the common people.

In other words, the majority of both groups looked upon Willkie as a business man's and Roosevelt as the working man's champion. But while the Democrats let it go at that, there was a strong tendency among the Republicans to stress that what is good for business is good for everyone or even to add a specific claim for Willkie as offering the most promising situation for the common people too. In short, the onus now rests upon a business candidate; he must somehow claim a connection with the people. No parallel obligation rests upon the candidate of the working people; he does not have to pretend to benefit business.

We now turn to a second source of data on the social attitudes of the two groups of voters: the arguments which people gave to explain their change in vote intention. If a respondent was found to have a vote intention different from the one he gave at his previous interview, he was asked the reasons for this change. The main emphasis in these detailed interviews was on tracing the influence of radio and newspaper. But in the course of their replies the respondents were bound to mention the arguments which had impressed them.[1]

More than a third of the Republicans and more than a quarter of the Democrats mentioned economic arguments as reasons for a change of vote. These arguments fell roughly into two groups. The majority of them were "class" arguments; one way or another they took a stand on the "poor man—rich man" issue. The other group had no readily apparent class character.

There were several ways of stating a class position. A "poor man's" argument might be approval of the WPA or a statement that Willkie favored big business or the contention that wages would go down if he were elected. A "rich man's" argument might be that Willkie would restore business confidence or that Roosevelt was ruining business or that he had undermined the self-reliance of workers by his unemployment policy.

The non-class arguments referred to farm matters; to an anticipated increase in general prosperity under one or the other candidate; to the inadequacy of the President's relief program; to the national debt and the excessive spending under the New Deal;[2] and they included several miscellaneous comments such as "FDR is creating class hatred."

Of people who mentioned economic arguments when they made changes favorable to the Republicans,[3] 49 mentioned class arguments and 48 non-class arguments. Among the Democrats, 73 made comments on economic issues which had a class character and only 12 did not. Incidentally, this shows once more that the Democrats were more inclined to think and argue in class terms. This does not mean that Democrats were more "class conscious" but rather that they did not experience social pressure to disguise their class interest.

The vital point for our present discussion is the clear-cut relationship between party and the content of economic argumentation (Table I). The Democrats, when they cited class argu-

TABLE I: NUMBER OF REPUBLICAN AND DEMOCRATIC CHANGERS MENTIONING CLASS ARGUMENTS

Type of Argument	Republicans	Democrats
Poor man's argument	14	73
Rich man's argument	35	0
Total class arguments	49	73

ments, usually used "poor man's" arguments exclusively. The Republicans stressed mainly the "rich man's" point of view. The 14 Republicans who explicitly stated that they changed to Willkie because his election would be beneficial to the worker and the common man are an interesting exception. They argued largely in general terms, saying that Willkie would be "for the working man," or that because he had worked his way up he would understand the needs of the working class. (The latter point, Willkie's humble beginnings, was made much of during the campaign and will be mentioned again later.)

For the future historian, the details of this kind of argumentation should be of great interest. The arguments can logically be classified in four groups: 1. My own candidate is for _____; 2. The other candidate is for _____; 3. The other candidate is against _____; 4. My own candidate is against _____. Out of the more than 100 comments we could draw on, there was not one case of Type 4, where a vote intention would be explained by a candidate's stand *against* something. The Democrats never said that Roosevelt was against big business or monopolies, and the Republicans never said Willkie would do away with the WPA or any other social legislation. In this election at least, people showed a reluctance to assign any aggressive tendencies to their own candidates.

The opposition's candidate is, of course, freely accused of being dangerous to specific groups in the population, in arguments of Type 3 above. But here a noteworthy distinction between the two parties comes to light. The Democrats argued twice as often in favor of Roosevelt's social program as they did against the danger they saw in Willkie's affiliation with big business. The Republicans, on the other hand, were inclined to point up Roosevelt's dangerous economic policies at least as often as they stressed Willkie's value for the business man.

In sum, whenever economic and social matters were referred to there was a clear class structure in the argumentation used by the partisans of the two candidates.

Political "Extroversion"

The second major difference in the attitudes of the supporters of the two parties can best be introduced by reporting on the following question which our panel was asked in August and then again in October: "If you had to choose for President between a man who has had mostly experience in government and a man who has had mostly experience in business, which would you choose?"

In October, 40% of the entire panel voted for government and 47% for business experience with 13% remaining undecided. (In August the figures were very similar—41%, 45% and 14% respectively.) The sample, therefore, divides fairly evenly on this issue, but there are sharp party differences (Chart 9).

The Republicans voted, in large majority, for the businessman while the Democrats, with practically the same frequency, preferred a presidential candidate with government experience. There are probably two factors which have to be drawn on in the interpretation of this result. One is that one of the two candidates had come from a business career, and the other one from a career as a public official. To a certain degree, therefore, their followers had to accept this distinction and make the best of it.

CHART 9

Republicans prefer a president with business experience, whereas Democrats think it more important to have a president with government experience.

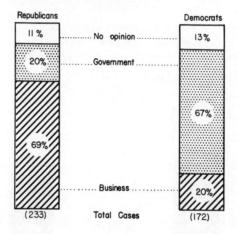

But at the same time, it is hardly a coincidence that the two standard bearers had such characteristically different pasts. Since the Civil War it has always been the Democratic presidents who symbolized the importance of government as a pursuit of its own. Grover Cleveland is associated with the first success in Civil Service reform. Woodrow Wilson was a professor of government and his notion of the "New Freedom" highlighted the role of government. Roosevelt's New Deal, finally, called for a completely new conception of our governmental institutions.

The Republican administrations in turn were always more concerned with business matters. After the Civil War they were the symbol of expansion toward the West. McKinley had to concentrate on monetary or tariff matters. The three Republican administrations after the World War were all elected on prosperity platforms, with Harding almost an anti-government candidate.[4] Coolidge thought that "the business of America was business," and Hoover was the "Great Engineer," a representative of successful mining enterprise. In short, the result in Chart 9 seems to represent the residual effect of a fairly consistent historical tradition.

CHART 10

In their conversations with friends, Republicans talked more about the campaign and less about the war than Democrats.

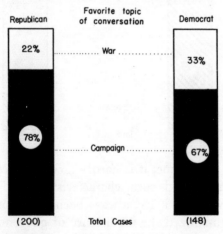

The idea might even be further generalized to the notion of social inclusiveness. We might think of political "extroverts" who take government more seriously than business and who give more weight to international than to national concerns. There is some indication in our material that the differences between the two parties extend to this broad field. In October our respondents were asked: "Do you talk with your friends more about the war or about the coming election?" Chart 10 shows the answers to this question among people who at the time had a Republican or a Democratic vote intention.

The Democrats were markedly more interested in the war than the Republicans. Thus according to our data, the Democrats were indeed more likely to be political extroverts, with a more inclusive viewpoint. They considered private business less important than public affairs, and were relatively more interested in the international scene than in domestic matters.

We have thus suggested two ideological differences between the two parties: (1) they take opposite sides on social issues and (2) they diverge along a hypothetical scale of political "extroversion" or social inclusiveness.[5]

The War in Europe

These differences are helpful in explaining a third and more temporary difference between the two parties in 1940: their attitude toward the European war.

The reader must still remember the climate of war discussion in the summer of 1940. The "phony war" had been succeeded by a series of shattering German victories. The question of American involvement became more and more acute. The conscription bill had been passed and the industrial defense program had started to gain momentum. Lend-lease was still to come, but the inclination of the Roosevelt administration to give aid to the Allies had become apparent. The America First Committee had begun to set its weight against this trend in our foreign policy. Whether isolationism was possible or desirable was the question of the day.

We have two sets of data which show that the Republican voters tended more toward the isolationist side and the Democrats less. One source is a score which we might call an index of pro-Allied activism and which is constructed on the cumulative basis used for the IPP in the preceding chapter. Two questions were used:

"At the present time, which of the following should the United States do about helping England—less than we are doing now, the same, or more than we are doing now but not get into the war?"

"How do you feel about the passage of the conscription bill —do you approve or disapprove?"

About 25% of the Republicans opposed both the conscription program and any increase of aid to Britain whereas only 11% of the Democrats took this "isolationist" position on both questions. The relationship becomes especially clear in the extremes. Of the 38 people who wanted the United States to give less help to England, 82% were Republicans; and of the 42 people who disapproved of the conscription bill after it was passed, again 82% were Republicans.

This split in opinion becomes even more apparent if we turn to our second series, the reasons which respondents with changing vote intentions offered to explain their change of mind. Forty-eight per cent of the Democratic changers and 26% of the Republicans referred to the war in their comments. But more than half of the Democratic comments were statements to the effect that one cannot dispense with Roosevelt's experience in view of the European crisis, although they did not take a stand on whether the United States should enter or stay out of the European war.

About three-fourths of the arguments which took a stand on this question stated a desire to stay out of the war and one-fourth did not. Those which did not—the "non-isolationist" arguments—for the most part actually expressed only the awareness that our participation in the war was inevitable and should be anticipated by a constructive program, rather than taking a clear-cut interventionist position.

It is here that the difference between the two parties becomes apparent (Table 11). The Republicans, in almost a solid block, stressed keeping America out of the war. The Democrats were strikingly more likely to see the war situation from the point of view of our possible involvement in it.

TABLE II: REASON FOR CHANGE WHICH PERMITTED A
CLASSIFICATION ON THE WAR ISSUE

	Isolationist Arguments	Non-Isolationist Arguments
Republicans	36	5
Democrats	28	19

Partisanship and Party Argumentation

This elaboration of the differences between the parties should not be taken to mean that all Democrats disagree on all issues with all Republicans. In late October, when the formal campaigning reached its most intense stage, only 25% of the respondents were in what might be called whole-hearted agreement with their own parties. That is, only that number held the "correct" attitude on all, or nearly all, of eight arguments made by both sides.[6] On the other hand, about 35% of the partisans were relatively lukewarm toward the arguments made by their own party. Republicans and Democrats ranked equally on this scale. In short, there was a good deal of political tolerance on the part of the voters. And this is made still more noteworthy in comparison with the partisanship with which the campaign managers presented their cases in print and on the air. As is evident in Chapter XIII, campaign propaganda was far more partisan than the mass of the people.

Another indication of this lenient attitude toward the campaign is provided by the changes in opinion of some Republicans toward Roosevelt just after the election. Even a week or so after Election Day, when the smoke of the campaign battles had hardly had time to clear away, 22% of the Republican voters had already bettered their opinion of Roosevelt, now that he had again been elected president. Most of the Republicans, of course, still maintained the opinion they had held before Election Day.

This relative tolerance in partisanship is partly explained by the fact that there are a few areas in campaign argumentation on which the two parties substantially agree. The major area of agreement dealt with the personalities of the candidates. In a list of eight arguments submitted to the respondents, there were two arguments dealing with personality characteristics:

"Roosevelt has great personal attractiveness, capacity for hard work, and keen intelligence."

"Willkie is a self-made small-town man who made his way by his genius for industrial organization."

Not only were these arguments the most widely accepted by the respondents. In addition, they were the *only* arguments accepted by more members of the opposition than disagreed with them. Even Republicans conceded that Roosevelt was intelligent and industrious and even Democrats admitted that Willkie was a success. Whatever the people may think of minor politicians, they apparently prefer to believe that the nominees for the highest office in the land are worthy men. This is one important factor that facilitates the post-election adjustment on the part of those who voted for the loser.

The Republicans and Democrats tended to agree about the personalities of the candidates. There were two other kinds of reaction to the issues of the campaign. On economic problems the partisans were intent on arguing back and forth since each side was convinced of the soundness of its own position. Not so, however, with another kind of argumentation. In this case there was no joining of the issue. Each side had its own good argument—which it stressed. And each side recognized the opposition's good argument—which it avoided.

The Republicans' good argument involved the third term tradition. The Democrats' good argument involved Roosevelt's experience in foreign affairs during a world crisis. On such arguments, the twain never met. There was hardly a Republican who did not mention the third term as a reason for his Republican vote. And there was hardly a Democrat who tried to justify the third term as such. They preferred to ignore the issue. Instead, the Democrats argued against the third term theme by emphasizing the indispensability of Roosevelt's experience in a world at war. And here it was the Republicans who were embarrassed for an answer. They did not argue that such experience was not desirable or necessary, or that Roosevelt really did not have it, or that Willkie did. They simply avoided the issue as such, and tried to compensate for it by stressing the dangers of the third term, experience or not.

This raises the question of how strongly the people felt about the election, and we turn now to that topic.

CHAPTER V

Participation in the Election

Now that the social structure and the ideology of the two parties have been established, we need to introduce one more way in which people can be characterized in order to set the stage fully for the later discussion of the effectiveness of campaign propaganda.

The people at whom the campaign is directed are like the audience of any performance. They attend differently. In the audience of a radio program, for example, there are those who have the radio turned on but who do not listen to it. Perhaps they are only waiting for their favorite program which comes on the air next. There are others, at the opposite extreme, who are giving the program their full attention. And then there are numerous intermediary stages of attending. In the same way, the people of Erie County and the country were reached by the campaign to different degrees. Some kind of index is necessary to help us classify our respondents according to the extent to which they were psychologically involved in the political events preceding the presidential election. How *interested* were they in the campaign?

All through the study we collected a variety of indicators by which our respondents' interest could be gauged. A careful study of all pertinent interrelationships was made to decide which was the best measure to use.[1] The conclusion reached by this analysis was that the respondent's self-rating was the best index we had of his interest. The question was: "Would you say you have a great deal of interest in the coming election, a moderate interest, a mild interest, or no interest at all?" And his answer was more closely related to his involvement in the political scene than any other test we could make. So we took his word for it. On the basis of the answers to this question, we can classify the respondents into three groups: great, medium (moderate and mild), and no interest.

This is actually not as naive as it may sound. It is not surprising that people's self-rating on interest stands up well under a series of tests of consistency and validity. For being interested is a clearly recognizable experience, as anyone knows who has ever been unable to put down a detective story or been bored to tears at a cocktail party. Given any two activities, we can frequently tell at once which is the more interesting for us. During the interviewing, this question was asked a total of 5,260 times, and there were only 62 "Don't knows," or 1.2%. In other words, the question made sense to almost everyone and almost everyone had a ready answer.

Furthermore, if the self-rating is justified, the classification of interest will be related to other activities—activities which would reasonably come under the heading of "interested behavior." Actually, we can show that people on a higher level of interest (a) had more opinions on issues involved in the election; (b) participated more in election events; and (c) exposed themselves more to the stream of political communications.

To present this best, we use again the technique of forming simple cumulative indices which were introduced at the end of Chapter III when we talked about political predispositions. The indices incidentally contain information secured at different periods during the study[2] and thus exemplify one of the advantages of the repeated interviewing technique. The indices can be used to answer the question: how do people on different interest levels differ as to breadth of opinion, participation in the election, and general exposure to propaganda? As the level of interest decreases, (a) the more frequent the "Don't know" answers to certain opinion questions, (b) the lower the index of participation and activity in the campaign, and (c)

CHART 11

The more interested people are in the election, the more opinions they have on political issues, the more actively they participate in a campaign, and the more they expose themselves to campaign propaganda.

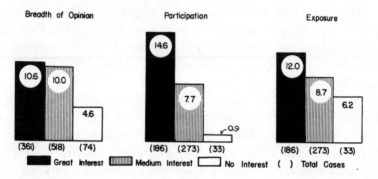

the less exposure to political communications (Chart 11).

Thus a reasonable relationship exists between the respondent's self-rating and the other components of what we call the "interest complex." And hence the interest rating is a valid classification device. To familiarize the reader with these interest levels, which will play a major role later, we now turn to some preliminary applications.

Who Are the Interested People?

Statistical results can be obtained only as answers to preceding speculations. The first possibility that comes to mind is the relationship between economic status and interest. Being poor means that few interests have been developed and that those which have been developed are in danger of becoming extinct as a result of repeated disappointments. Hence we would expect people on lower SES levels to be less interested in the election. Formal education is, of course, a direct creator of interest. But economic status and education are themselves highly related. Therefore to appraise the two factors correctly we have to study their effective influence simultaneously.

Education and SES level seem to have about equal importance in creating and maintaining political interest (Chart 12). If both are high, one-third the people express great interest in the election; if both are low, this proportion goes down to a fifth. In the middle range the two factors approximately compensate one another.

Differences of interest between rural and urban areas are not as great as the stereotype of the isolated farmer might lead one to expect. About 30% of the urban population and 23% of those on farms or in towns of fewer than 2,500 population rated

CHART 12

Both SES level and education affect interest in the election. The poor, uneducated voters show the lowest interest, and the more prosperous, educated ones the highest. The two middle groups reveal that SES level and education have about the same influence upon interest in the election.

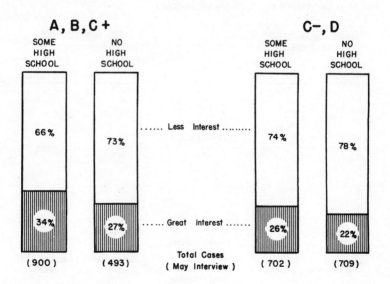

themselves on the highest level of interest. This may be peculiar to Erie County. The inhabitants of the urban center of Sandusky were not generally different from their neighbors on the farms because Sandusky is not a metropolis; and the surrounding farm area, on the other hand, was highly developed.

In determining the role of age, we must control the factor of education. In the last few decades the general level of education has greatly increased in this country. As a result, the younger generation has a higher educational level on the average than the older generation. Therefore, in order to appraise the influence of age we must deal with it separately on at least two educational levels.

On each educational level the older people are more interested in the election than the younger ones (Chart 13). This is a result which should not be passed by lightly. Is it desirable

CHART 13[3]

Older people have more interest in the election than younger.
This difference is especially marked with educated people,
but is still visible with the uneducated.

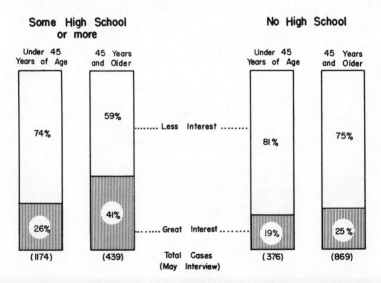

that younger people withdraw from the political scene? This might make for a greater stability of political life but at the same time it might also deprive it of a certain amount of energy and vitality and, thus, be regrettable from the standpoint of civic improvement. At any rate, the difference between American and European experience in this regard is clear; in pre-war Europe political movements on the part of youth were very active.

There is a prevailing belief that women are less interested in politics than men. This is corroborated by our data. In the May poll, 33% of the men but only 23% of the women professed great interest in the election.

In short, the person most interested in the election is more likely to be found in urban areas among men on higher levels of education, with better socio-economic status, and among older age groups.

Least Participation in the Campaign—the Non-Voter

The acid test for interest in the election is actual voting. In 1940 Erie County had the high voting record of 81%. This was almost perfectly reflected in our panel, where 82% of the 511 people finally interviewed reported that they had actually voted.

The greatest proportion of non-voters was indeed found on the lowest interest level. People with no interest in the election were 18 times as likely not to vote as people with great interest (Chart 14).

Non-voting is a serious problem in a democracy. It is therefore worthwhile to look at these non-voters somewhat more closely. The great majority of them were *deliberate* non-voters; in October, during the last interview before the election, 29% intended to vote and knew for whom they would vote, 7% intended to vote but did not yet know for whom, and 64% did not intend to vote. In other words, two out of three cases of non-voting were intentional and premeditated, according to the voters' own statements. But even in the other

CHART 14

Non-voting is a function of the level of interest.

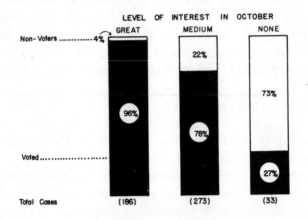

LEVEL   OF   INTEREST   IN   OCTOBER

| GREAT | MEDIUM | NONE |

Non-Voters 4%

Voted....................

Total Cases   (186)   (273)   (33)

groups there were some non-voters who resembled the pre-meditated ones.

Of the people who did not carry through their preceding vote intention, only one-half had a legitimate reason: they were ill or had made a mistake about registration rules. The other half had never been interested in the elections and the reasons they gave were not at all convincing: "too busy sorting apples," "there were too many people waiting at the polls," and so on.

A few people could not decide how to vote right up to the last moment. Half of them liked or disliked the candidates equally, so they finally decided not to vote at all. The other half had such low interest records throughout the sequence of interviews and offered so little to explain their indecision that they, too, would be more aptly labelled deliberate non-voters. On the other hand, a few people in the group of deliberate non-voters were not without interest in the election; they saw no difference between the two candidates or they felt that voting is no remedy for current social ills.

As a net result, three-quarters of the non-voters stayed away from the polls deliberately because they were thoroughly unconcerned with the election. This sheds a new light on the whole problem of the non-voter. Only a small number of people were kept from the polls by a last minute emergency. The possibility that the deliberate non-voters could have been made more interested during the campaign is slight; their decision not to vote was too persistent. A long range program of civic education would be needed to draw such people into the orbit of political life, and further studies are needed to unearth the specific nature of their lack of interest.

If we push the analysis of our own data a step further, we gain additional insight into the problem. Perhaps some primary personal characteristics are involved. But the difference in deliberate non-voting between people with more or less education can be completely accounted for by the notion of interest.

Once the interest level is kept constant, education does not make any further difference (Chart 15). Deliberate non-voting

CHART 15[4]

Once the interest level is held constant, education does not affect the proportion of non-voters.

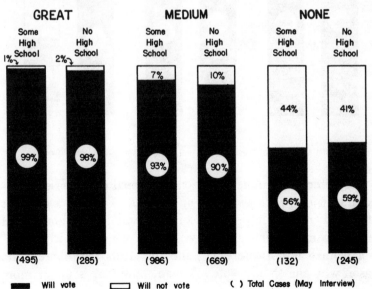

GREAT		MEDIUM		NONE	
Some High School	No High School	Some High School	No High School	Some High School	No High School
1%	2%	7%	10%	44%	41%
99%	98%	93%	90%	56%	59%
(495)	(285)	(986)	(669)	(132)	(245)

■ Will vote   ☐ Will not vote   ( ) Total Cases (May Interview)

increases greatly as interest decreases—but if a person is interested, he will vote irrespective of his formal educational level. On the other hand, if he is not interested, he is not likely to vote in any case.

A similar picture is obtained for people on different SES levels, for those with different residences, and for different age and religion groups. But the result is startlingly different for the sex of the respondents (Chart 16).

CHART 16

Sex is the only personal characteristic which affects non-voting, even if interest is held constant. Men are better citizens but women are more reasoned: if they are not interested, they do not vote.

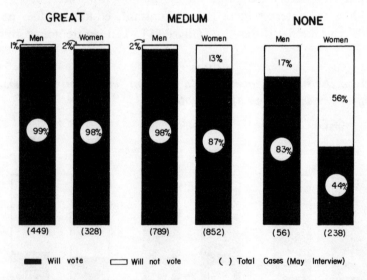

Sex differences, alone among the personal characteristics, affect non-voting *independently of interest*. The less a group is interested in the election, the greater will be the amount of deliberate non-voting among women as compared with men. If a woman is not interested, she just feels that there is no reason why she should vote. A man, however, is under more social pressure and will therefore go to the polls even if he is not "interested" in the events of the campaign. Not only is it true that women feel no compulsion to vote, but some of them actually consider their aloofness a virtue. Remarks such as these were not infrequent:

"I don't care to vote. Voting is for the men."

"I think men should do the voting and the women should stay home and take care of their work."

"I have never voted. I never will. . . . A woman's place is in the home. . . . Leave politics to the men."

In other words, although legal restrictions upon women's participation in politics were removed some twenty-five years ago, the attitude of women toward politics has not yet brought them to full equality with men. Changes in the mores have lagged behind changes in legislation.

In summary, then, efforts to extend political participation will have to overcome the general indifference to current affairs which seems characteristic for a part of the population. In addition, however, such efforts must refute the idea that public life is, by common consent, the man's realm.

Most Participation in the Campaign—the Opinion Leaders

The non-voters represent the low point in political participation. The high point is illustrated by the people most active in a presidential campaign—the "opinion leaders." Common observation and many community studies show that in every area and for every public issue there are certain people who are most concerned about the issue as well as most articulate about it. We call them the "opinion leaders."

The opinion leaders of a community could best be identified and studied by asking people to whom they turn for advice on the issue at hand and then investigating the interaction between the advisers and the advisees. It is obvious that in a study involving a sample, like the present one, that procedure would be extremely difficult if not impossible since few of the related leaders and "followers" would happen to be included within the sample. As a substitute device, however, we can identify the opinion leaders and the followers within our panel, without relating them directly to one another.

At about the middle of the campaign, the respondents were asked these two questions:

"Have you tried to convince anyone of your political ideas recently?"

"Has anyone asked your advice on a political question recently?"

All those people who answered "Yes" to either or both of these questions—21% of the entire group—were designated as opinion leaders. Their responses to other questions during the series of interviews as well as subsequent check-ups on their objective roles within certain groups established the validity of the identification. In short, the opinion leaders are substantially representative of that aggressive section of the community—or rather, the aggressive sections of the several sub-communities—which tried to influence the rest of the community.

In connection with this last, one important matter must be emphasized: the opinion leaders are not identical with the socially prominent people in the community or the richest people or the civic leaders. They are found in all occupational groups (Table III).

TABLE III: PROPORTION OF OPINION LEADERS AND OTHERS
IN VARIOUS OCCUPATIONS

Occupation	Cases	Opinion Leaders %	Others %
Professional	17	35	65
Proprietary, managerial	28	25	75
Clerical	21	33	67
Commercial, sales	16	44	56
Skilled workers	37	35	65
Semi-skilled workers	31	32	68
Unskilled workers	47	23	77
Farmers	46	15	85
Housewives	230	13	87
Unemployed	13	15	85
Retired	23	35	65

In all respects, the opinion leaders demonstrated greater political alertness. Whereas only 24% of the "followers" professed a great deal of interest in the election, fully 61% of the opinion leaders rated themselves thus. Similarly in exposure to political communications: on each level of interest, the opinion leaders read and listened to campaign material much more than the non-opinion leaders (Table IV). What is more, the opinion leaders who considered their interest only "moderate" or "mild" still managed to read and listen more than the non-opinion leaders who thought they were "greatly interested." In addition, they talked politics more than the others. Fully 90% of the opinion leaders conversed about the campaign with their associates just before our October interview whereas only 58% of the others had done so.

TABLE IV: INDEX OF EXPOSURE OF OPINION LEADERS AND OTHERS TO THE FORMAL MEDIA OF COMMUNICATION

	Great Interest		Less Interest	
	OLs	Others	OLs	Others
Newspaper	15.8	12.3	14.8	6.6
Radio	14.6	12.3	13.0	7.6
Magazine	20.6	14.1	15.8	4.6

In all important respects, then, the opinion leaders were the most responsive to campaign events.[5] In a later part of this report, we will return to the specific role which these opinion leaders played in the course of the campaign.

Now that we have established the factor of interest in the election, which will be used frequently in the following chapters, we can turn to the section of the population which stands in the center of attention: the people who formed their final vote intention during the course of the campaign itself.

CHAPTER VI

Time of Final Decision

All during an election campaign, people can make up their minds. Many traditional party voters, however, know far in advance of the campaign for whom they will vote. It might be possible now to forecast the party for which Southerners will vote in 1960, although the issue and candidates will not be known for fifteen years. Others decide during a particular term of office whether they will support the incumbent and his party at the next election. Many know in May, even before candidates are nominated, how they will vote in November.

Interviews with the panel permitted us to distinguish three kinds of voters classified according to the time when they made their *final vote decision* — the decision which they followed throughout the rest of the campaign and in the voting booth.

"May Voters": These pre-campaign deciders knew in May, at our first interview, how they would vote, maintained their choice throughout the campaign, and actually voted for that choice in November. Their votes had been finally determined by May.

"June-to-August Voters": These people settled upon a candidate during the convention period (our August interview was the first interview after both conventions), maintained their choice throughout the rest of the campaign, and actually voted for that choice in November. Their votes were finally determined in June, July or August.

"September-to-November Voters": These people did not definitely make up their minds until the last few months of the campaign, some of them not until Election Day itself. Their

votes were finally determined only in September, October or November.

What were the significant differences between these groups of people? Why did some people make up their minds before the campaign began, others during the first months of the campaign, and still others not until the end of the campaign?

The analysis in this chapter develops two major factors influencing the time of final decision. First, the people whose decision was delayed had *less interest* in the election. Second, those who made their choice in the late days of the campaign were people subject to *more cross-pressures*. By "cross-pressures" we mean the conflicts and inconsistencies among the factors which influence vote decision. Some of these factors in the environment of the voter may influence him toward the Republicans while others may operate in favor of the Democrats. In other words, cross-pressures upon the voter drive him in opposite directions.

Interest and Time of Decision

The more interested people were in the election, the sooner they definitely decided how they would vote. Almost two-thirds of the voters with great interest had already made up their minds by May; but considerably less than half of the voters with less interest in the election had made up their minds by May (Chart 17).[1] Only one-eighth of the greatly interested waited until the late period of the campaign before finally deciding how they would vote; twice as many of the less interested delayed their decision until that period.

The general tendency for late decision among the less interested held for both parties (Chart 18). But on each level of interest, the Democrats tended to decide later than the Republicans.

Certain other manifestations of interest also wane in the group whose decision is postponed until the later stages of a campaign. At one point respondents were asked whether they were "very anxious" to see their candidate elected, whether it

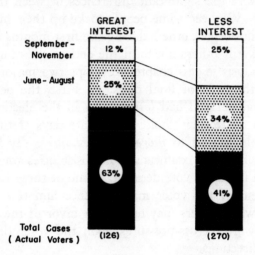

CHART 17

People greatly interested in the election make their final vote decision earlier than less interested people.

	GREAT INTEREST	LESS INTEREST
September–November	12 %	25%
June–August	25%	34%
Total Cases (Actual Voters)	63% (126)	41% (270)

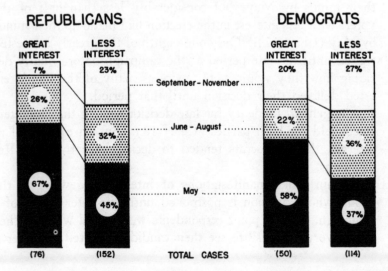

CHART 18

It is true for both parties: the higher the interest, the earlier the decision is likely to be made.

REPUBLICANS   **DEMOCRATS**

	GREAT INTEREST	LESS INTEREST		GREAT INTEREST	LESS INTEREST
September–November	7%	23%		20%	27%
June–August	26%	32%		22%	36%
May	67%	45%		58%	37%
TOTAL CASES	(76)	(152)		(50)	(114)

was "not terribly important" although "I would like to see my candidate elected," or whether "it doesn't make much difference."

The particular persons who were "very anxious" to have their candidate win were those who decided on their vote early in the campaign (Chart 19). The same reasons which impelled them to choose a candidate early in the game and stick with him also served to make them quite concerned about his election. The people who were not particularly concerned about the outcome of the election were those who decided late in the campaign. They felt that nothing much was at stake and waited for happenstance or friends to make up their minds for them. As the campaign moved on, the respondents who answered "don't know" were also saying in effect "don't care."

The campaign managers were thus continuously faced with the task of propagandizing not only a steadily shrinking seg-

CHART 19

The partisans who are "very anxious" to have their candidate elected make their final vote decision early in the campaign. Those who are not much concerned as to who wins decide only later.

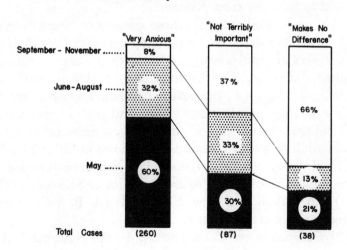

ment of the electorate but also a segment whose interest in and concern with the election also steadily shrank. By the end of the campaign, the managers were exerting their greatest efforts to catch the few votes of the least interested and least involved persons.

Cross-Pressures and Time of Decision

In Chapter III, we indicated that there were a number of factors differentiating Republican and Democratic voters. Each of these factors could be considered a "pressure" upon final vote decision. We found the Protestant vote allied to the Republicans and the Catholic vote more strongly Democratic. We found that individuals on the higher SES levels tended to vote Republican and their poorer neighbors to vote Democratic. In other words, a vote decision can be considered the net effect of a variety of pressures.

Now what if these individual factors work in opposite directions? Suppose an individual is *both* prosperous and Catholic? How will he make up his mind? Or suppose he belongs to the Protestant faith and lives in a poor section of the community? Which of the conflicting influences will win out? People who are subject to contradictory and opposing influences of this kind are said to be under cross-pressures.

The more evenly balanced these opposing pressures were, the longer the voter delayed in making up his mind. We shall use six instances of cross-pressures to show their effect in delaying the time of decision. The first three cases involve personal characteristics of the voter; the next two, relationships between the voter and other people around him; and the last, the voter's basic political attitudes. The effect of cross-pressures of all six types in delaying final vote decision is shown in Chart 20.

(1) *Religion and SES Level:* The first cross-pressure we have already mentioned. Protestants on lower SES levels (C— & D) and Catholics on upper SES levels (A, B, & C+) were subject to this cross-pressure.

(2) *Occupation and Identification:* In the November inter-

view respondents were asked with what groups in the community they identified themselves—big business, small business, labor, etc. While most people identified themselves with the class to which they would have been assigned by occupation, some semi-skilled and unskilled workers tended to think of themselves as belonging with the business class and a few white-collar people thought of themselves as belonging with labor. Since the business group ordinarily supported one party and the labor group the other, a cross-pressure was set up between the voter's objective occupation and his subjective identification.

(3) *1936 Vote and 1940 Vote:* Most of the people—but again not all of them—voted for the same party in both presidential elections. The voters who changed between the 1936 and the 1940 elections—primarily made up of persons who had voted for Roosevelt in 1936 but were for Willkie in 1940—could be regarded as having something of a tradition to overcome. Their way was psychologically more obstructed than that of the people who voted consistently for the same party in all recent elections.

(4) *The Voter and His Family:* As we shall see, the American family maintains considerable political solidarity, with all adult members voting the same way. But sometimes other members of the respondent's family disagreed with him and oftener other members of the family were undecided. In either case, the respondent was under a cross-pressure between the views of two members of the family or between his own ideas and those of at least one other member of his family.

(5) *The Voter and His Associates:* Friends as well as family create a political environment which may be congenial or hostile. In the October interviews, respondents were asked whether they had noticed changes in vote intention on the part of people around them. Republicans who noted a trend toward Willkie and Democrats who were aware mainly of changes toward Roosevelt were in a congenial situation. What they saw going on around them coincided with their own preferences. But the few who noticed trends towards the opposition party were sub-

CHART 20

People who are exposed to cross-pressures delay their final vote decision. This is true separately for people with great interest and for those with less interest. The effect of the cross-pressure is illustrated in each pair of bars. This chart represents those with great interest.

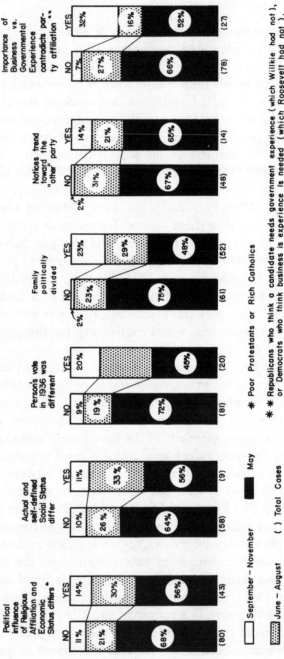

| Political influence of Religious Affiliation and Economic Status differs * | | Actual and self-defined Social Status differ | | Person's vote in 1936 was different | | Family politically divided | | Notices trend toward the "other" party | | Importance of Business vs. Governmental Experience contradicts party affiliation ** | |

NO / YES sections:

Political influence of Religious Affiliation and Economic Status differs *
- NO (80): 11%, 21%, 68%
- YES (43): 14%, 30%, 56%

Actual and self-defined Social Status differ
- NO (58): 10%, 26%, 64%
- YES (9): 11%, 33%, 56%

Person's vote in 1936 was different
- NO (81): 9%, 19%, 72%
- YES (20): 20%, 45%

Family politically divided
- NO (61): 2%, 23%, 75%
- YES (52): 23%, 29%, 49%

Notices trend toward the "other" party
- NO (48): 2%, 31%, 67%
- YES (14): 14%, 21%, 65%

Importance of Business vs. Governmental Experience contradicts party affiliation **
- NO (78): 7%, 27%, 66%
- YES (27): 32%, 16%, 52%

☐ September – November   ■ June – August   ( ) Total Cases
☐ May

* Poor Protestants or Rich Catholics

** Republicans who think a candidate needs government experience (which Willkie had not), or Democrats who think business is experience is needed (which Roosevelt had not).

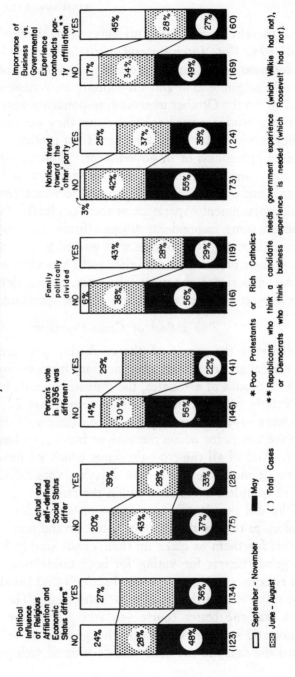

(CONTINUATION OF CHART 20)

This chart represents those with less interest.

Political Influence of Religious Affiliation and Economic Status differs *

NO	YES
(123)	(134)
24%	27%
28%	
48%	36%

Actual and self-defined Social Status differ

NO	YES
(75)	(28)
20%	39%
43%	28%
37%	33%

Person's vote in 1936 was different

NO	YES
(146)	(41)
14%	29%
30%	
56%	22%

Family politically divided

NO	YES
(116)	(119)
6%	
38%	43%
56%	28%
	29%

Notices trend toward the "other" party

NO	YES
(73)	(24)
3%	25%
42%	37%
55%	38%

Importance of Business vs. Governmental Experience contradicts party affiliation **

NO	YES
(169)	(60)
17%	45%
34%	28%
49%	27%

□ September – November
■ May
▒ June – August
( ) Total Cases

* Poor Protestants or Rich Catholics

** Republicans who think a candidate needs government experience is needed (which Willkie had not), or Democrats who think business experience is needed (which Roosevelt had not).

jected thereby to conflicting pressures from their associates.

(6) *1940 Vote Intention and Attitude Toward Business and Government:* And, finally, cross-pressures may exist between a person's vote intention and his attitude on a basic issue of the election. In the October interview, respondents were questioned on their attitudes toward one such issue: they were asked whether they considered it more important for a president to have experience in business or in government. Most people with Republican vote intentions wanted a president with business experience and most people who intended to vote Democratic preferred government experience in their candidate. There were, however, some respondents whose attitude and vote intention were conflicting—Republicans who wanted government experience in their presidential candidate and Democrats who thought business experience was more important. These deviates, then, were subject to a certain amount of cross-pressure.

The Effect of Cross-Pressures

Whatever the source of the conflicting pressures, whether from social status or class identification, from voting traditions or the attitudes of associates, the consistent result was to delay the voter's final decision. As shown in Chart 20, the voters who were subject to cross-pressures on their vote decided later than the voters for whom the various factors reinforced one another. And of all the cross-pressures which we have identified the single most effective one in delaying vote decision was the lack of complete agreement within the family.

Why did people subject to cross-pressures delay their final decisions as to how they should vote? In the first place, it was difficult for them to make up their minds simply because they had good reasons for voting for both candidates. Sometimes such reasons were so completely balanced that the decision had to be referred to a third factor for settlement. The doubt as to which was the better course—to vote Republican or to vote Democratic — combined with the process of self-argument caused the delay in the final vote decision of such people.

In the second place, some of the people subject to cross-pressures delayed their final vote decisions because they were waiting for events to resolve the conflicting pressures. In the case of conflicting personal characteristics, such resolution was hardly possible but in other cases a reconciliation of conflicting interests might be anticipated. A person might hope that during the campaign he could convince other members of his family, or even more, he might give the family every chance to bring him around to their way of thinking. And the family often does just that. Or, again, he might wait for events in the campaign to provide him with a basis for making up his mind. Although there is a tendency toward consistency in attitudes, sometimes the contradiction was not resolved and the voter actually went to the polls with the cross-pressures still in operation.

Such conflicting pressures make voters "fair game" for the campaign managers of both parties, for they have a foot in each party. They are subject to factors which influence them to vote Republican and others, perhaps equally strong, which influence them to vote Democratic.

From this particular point of view, the heavy campaigning of both parties at the end of the campaign is a good investment for both sides—to the extent to which it can be effective at all. We will recall that the people who make up their minds last are those who think the election will affect them least. It may be, then, that explicit attempts by the candidates and their managers to prove to them that the election *will* make a difference to them would be more effective than any amount of continued argumentation of the issues as such. One hypothesis is that the person or the party that convinces the hesitant voter of the importance of the election to him personally—in terms of what he concretely wants—can have his vote.

Interest and Cross-Pressures

How are interest and cross-pressures inter-related? Remembering that controversy often makes issues exciting, we might expect that those for whom the decision is difficult would become most involved with and concerned about the election. But that would leave out of the reckoning a basic pattern of human adjustment. When people desire and shun a course of action in about equal degree, they often do not decide for or against it but rather change the subject or avoid the matter altogether. For many clashes of interest, the easy way to get out of the uncomfortable situation is simply to discount its importance and to give up the conflict as not worth the bother.[2]

Thus, many voters subject to cross-pressures tended to belittle the whole affair. They escaped from any real conflict by losing interest in the election. They had no clear-cut stake in the victory of either candidate. Thus they were relatively indifferent as to who won, and the election became less important to them and less interesting. Those with no cross-pressures showed most interest in the election; even one cross-pressure meant a substantial increase in the proportion of voters who felt less interested in the election. And, as the number of cross-pressures increases, the degree of interest shows a steady decline (Chart 21).

CHART 21

As cross-pressures increase, the amount of interest in the election decreases.

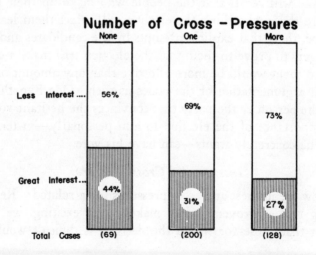

Number of Cross – Pressures

	None	One	More
Less Interest	56%	69%	73%
Great Interest...	44%	31%	27%
Total Cases	(69)	(200)	(128)

Given that the two factors bear such an inverse relationship to one another, how do they work jointly to affect the time of final decision? Is one more important than the other?

Naturally, the people who made up their minds first were the people who *could* make them up with the least difficulty and who had the most incentive for doing so—i.e., the people with no or one cross-pressure in voting background and with great interest in the election (Chart 22). Fully three-fourths of them knew in May how they would vote in November, while only 7% of them waited until the last weeks of the campaign before settling their vote intention once and for all. At the other extreme were the people subject to two or more cross-pressures and without much interest in the election. Only one-fourth of them made a final decision as early as May and fully one-third waited until the last period of the campaign before finally making up their minds.

CHART 22

Both cross-pressures and lack of interest delay the final vote decision. Their joint effect is especially strong. Separately, they show about equal strength.

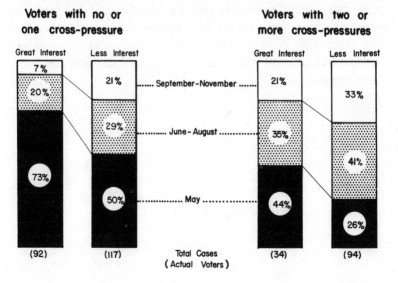

Voters with no or one cross-pressure		Voters with two or more cross-pressures	
Great Interest	Less Interest	Great Interest	Less Interest

September–November: 7%, 21%, 21%, 33%

June–August: 20%, 29%, 35%, 41%

May: 73%, 50%, 44%, 26%

(92)   (117)   Total Cases (Actual Voters)   (34)   (94)

But what of the people with one of the factors favorable to an early decision and the other unfavorable, i.e., those with several cross-pressures and great interest and those with no or one cross-pressure and less interest? These middle-of-the-roaders do not differ from each other in the time at which they made their final decision. In other words, when the two factors—interest and cross-pressures—work in opposing directions, they are about equal in strength.

The comparison between cross-pressures and lack of interest is not fully expressed in these quantitative statements. There are qualitative differences in response as well. If the voter faces a clear-cut situation, free from cross-pressures, then interest determines how soon his practically inevitable decision will be precipitated. Awareness of the election is paralleled at once by recognition of his "natural" position. If the voter happens to be faced by cross-pressures, then interest operates a little differently. Where interest is not too strong, the tendency is to dismiss the whole issue as not making very much difference. The line of least resistance is not to vote at all, and many such people do not vote. Strong interest may overcome the impulse to avoid the matter and keep the prospective but puzzled voter arguing the case with himself and his friends until Election Day forces a decision or some incident serves to swing the close balance of decision. Great interest tends to bring a decision *as such* whereas lack of conflicting pressures brings a decision *for* one or the other party.

CHAPTER VII

The Types of Changes

People delayed their final vote decisions either because they did not have enough interest in the election to push through to a definite choice or because the selection of a candidate put them in a difficult situation, containing elements favorable to both sides. But the process of delay did not work identically for all of them. Some people were "Don't Know's" until sometime during the campaign and then definitely decided on their vote. Others decided early in the campaign for one of the candidates, then had a period of doubt when they became undecided or even went over to the other side, and finally came back to the original choice. Still others changed from one particular party to the other. In short, the people who did not make up their minds until some time during the campaign proper differed in the ways in which they came to their final vote decision. In this sense, the three main kinds of changers were the following (the figures are percentages of the voters as a whole):[1]

28% Crystallizers: They are people who had no vote intention in May but later acquired one; they went from "Don't Know" to Republican (14%) or from "Don't Know" to Democrat (14%).

15% Waverers: They are people who started out with a vote intention, then fell away from it (either to "Don't Know" or to the other party) and later returned to their original choice. Most of them went from a party to "Don't Know" and then back to the original party (11%: Republicans, 5.5%; Democrats, 5.5%), and others from a party to the other party and then back to the first party (4%: Republicans, 1%; Democrats, 3%).

8% Party Changers: They are people who started out with a vote intention and later changed to the other party, finally voting for it. They went from Republican to Democrat (2%) or from Democrat to Republican (6%).

We might note now, for use later, that all the changes of the crystallizers and most of the waverers involved only one of the parties; the other part of the change was a "Don't Know" opinion. On the other hand, all the party changers and some of the waverers were at one time or another in the camp of each party; their changes involved allegiance to both parties at different times. In other words, 39% of the changes made by the voters involved only one party and only 12% of them involved both parties. Or, adding the constants from May to November, the vote intentions of 88% of all the voters were limited to one party and the vote intentions of only 12% of the voters took in both parties, at one time or another.

Of the waverers who left their original choice for indecision, fully 82% returned to it as the more congenial home. But those who wandered away to the other party did not return so readily; only 32% came back to the party of their first choice. If a person leaves his party for indecision he almost always returns to it later, but if he leaves it for the opposition, he seldom returns to it.

Time of Final Decision and the Changers

As the campaign wore on, what kinds of changers were still left to be convinced, once and for all?

The three kinds of changers—the crystallizers, the waverers, and the party changers—all came to their final decision sometime after May, but not all at the same time. Actually, the crystallizers decided much earlier than the others; 68% had settled their vote by August as against only 48% of the party changers and 46% of the waverers.

But the waverers—the people who left the party of their

original choice but later came back and voted for it—comprise a special group because, as we noted above, there were two different kinds of waverers. There were those who wavered only to indecision and there were those who wavered all the way to the other party. This "distance" of the wavering is significant both for time of final decision and, as we shall see, for the roles of interest and cross-pressures. The indecision waverers definitely decided much earlier than the party waverers (57% by August as against 14%). If, then, we divide the changers into two groups—the one-party changers (crystallizers and indecision waverers) and the two-party changers (the straight party changers and the party waverers)—we find that the people who intended sometime during the campaign to vote for both parties took much longer to reach a final vote decision than those who varied only between one of the parties and indecision (Chart 23). Almost two-thirds of the two-party changers did not definitely decide until the last period of the campaign; almost two-thirds of the one-party changers definitely decided by August. As the campaign went into its last weeks, the people who were still to make up their minds, relatively speaking, were those who had been in the camp of the opposition earlier.

Interest, Cross-Pressures, and the Changers

What were the roles of interest in the election and cross-pressures in voting background for these groups of voters who had arrived at their final vote decision in different ways? Did these two influential factors differentiate such voters?[2]

The story is clear. There was a steady decrease of interest and a steady increase of cross-pressures from constants to one-party changers to two-party changers. The people who changed their position during the campaign but never enough to move into both parties stood between the constants and the two-party people. In other words, the more interest and the fewer conflicting pressures a person had, the more he tended to decide once and for all early in the game and never change his mind thereafter (Chart 24). If a person had somewhat less interest

CHART 23

People who vary only between a party and indecision decide their vote earlier than those who vary between both parties.

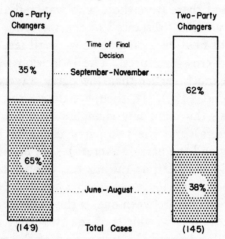

One - Party Changers

Two - Party Changers

Time of Final Decision

September - November ...... 35% / 62%

65% / 38%

...... June - August ......

(149)   Total Cases   (145)

CHART 24

The less interest people have and the more cross-pressures to which they are subject, the more variable are their vote intentions.

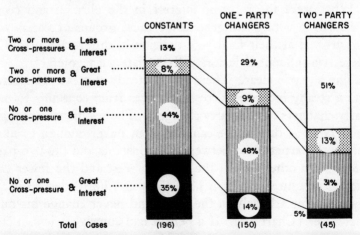

		CONSTANTS	ONE - PARTY CHANGERS	TWO - PARTY CHANGERS
Two or more Cross-pressures &	Less Interest	13%	29%	51%
Two or more Cross-pressures &	Great Interest	8%	9%	
No or one Cross-pressure &	Less Interest	44%	48%	13%
No or one Cross-pressure &	Great Interest	35%	14%	31%
				5%
Total Cases		(196)	(150)	(45)

and somewhat more cross-pressures, then he tended to doubt longer and oftener than the constants but he slid back only to a tentative "don't know" and never far enough to get into the other camp. Only those people who had much less interest and many more conflicting pressures actually vacillated between the two parties.[3]

That tells the story of the two-party changers: they were the people who were torn in both directions and who did not have enough interest in the election to cut through the conflicting pressures upon them and come to a deliberate and definite decision. Instead, they drifted along during the campaign, drifting into both parties. They not only delayed longer than any other group of voters in making their final vote decision but when they did make it, as we shall see, they were as likely as not to be swayed by someone in their immediate environment. These people, who in a sense were the only ones of the entire electorate to make a complete change during the campaign were: the least interested in the election; the least concerned about its outcome; the least attentive to political material in the formal media of communication; the last to settle upon a vote decision; and the most likely to be persuaded, finally, by a personal contact, not an "issue" of the election.

In short, the party changers—relatively, the people whose votes still remained to be definitely determined during the last stages of the campaign, the people who could swing an election during those last days—were, so to speak, available to the person who saw them last before Election Day. The notion that the people who switch parties during the campaign are mainly the reasoned, thoughtful, conscientious people who were convinced by the issues of the election is just plain wrong. Actually, they were mainly just the opposite.

The Personality Traits of the Changers

The personalities of the different kinds of voters can be compared on the basis of ratings made by our interviewers. After the fourth interview, by which time the interviewers had become reasonably well acquainted with the respondents, each member of the panel was rated on a graphic rating scale covering ten personality characteristics readily observed during interviews.

On almost all traits, the constants were rated superior to voters who changed in any way. Constants were reported to be more self-assured, better informed, more cooperative, and broader in their interests. All the traits correspond to their greater enthusiasm for the political campaign. All the changers, on the other hand, showed a limited range of community contacts and interests in their personality ratings as well as in other measures indicated previously. This underlines the finding that the campaign itself is progressively waged in order to win the less interested and less involved, the "withdrawn" individuals living within narrower horizons.

The waverers were distinguished by a higher rating on "fair-mindedness" which probably grew directly out of their hesitation and reservations. In addition, the waverers seemed to suffer somewhat more from emotional maladjustment as evidenced in more unhappiness and lack of self-assurance. It is a well-known psychological pattern for uneasiness to lead to floundering about in areas not directly related to the distress.

The ratings on the party changers indicated that the direction of the change has to be taken into account. There were no personality characteristics which distinguished the party changers as such. In personality, the party changers resembled the adherents of the party they changed *to* more than the adherents of the party they changed *from*. As we shall see, this is also true for other social variables.

The Mutability of the Changers

If various factors were sufficient to change people's minds once, perhaps they also served to change them again and again. This was exactly the case. At any particular time, voters who had changed their vote intentions previously were more likely to change again. In all, 59% of the changes made by voters throughout the entire campaign were made by only 38% of the changers (who were in turn only 19% of all the voters). This concentration of multiple changes in a relatively few people can be illustrated in another way. For each interview we can classify the voters into two groups: those who made a change of any sort at that time and those who did not. The voters who changed were three times as likely to change on the next interview as those who did not.

Such mutability represents only an extension of the influence of interest and cross-pressures. The people who found it difficult to distinguish between the virtues of the two parties and who at the same time were not sufficiently interested in the election to push their way through to a definite decision were more subject to the currents of campaign influence and hence were more changeable.

The Story of the Changers

All the changers definitely made up their minds sometime between June and November. But different times, different influences. The first influence upon the changers as a whole came in June, with the fall of France. The repercussions of that turn in the European war were strongly favorable to the Democrats. Of the people who definitely decided their vote in June, two-thirds decided for the Democrats, mainly on the ground that the European crisis necessitated the continuance of an experienced administration in Washington.

Then came the conventions, and the final vote decisions reached in July and August were mostly attributable to them. Voters who decided after the Republican convention were largely attracted to Willkie whereas those who decided after the Democratic convention divided more evenly between the parties but still favored the Republicans somewhat more. As a whole, then, the convention period helped the Republicans. On the one hand, the Republicans held a dramatic convention in which the dark-horse Willkie came to the fore in a striking finish whereas on the other hand the Democrats held what was generally regarded as a mismanaged and flat meeting which broke a major American precedent in nominating a third term candidate. As a result, the voters were attracted by the Republican convention and nomination but not by the Democratic. Finally, of all the people who changed to or from a party during the convention period, not one mentioned either party's platform or either vice-presidential nominee as a reason for change. The third term and the candidates themselves were the "issues" that dominated the reasons for change.

During the last weeks of the campaign, there were no events comparable in influence to the fall of France and the party conventions. During this late period, the two parties received roughly their proportionate share of votes. We now turn to the processes which affected the distribution of the shares.

The Process of Activation

Perhaps a few analogies will help to bring out the meaning of the concept of activation. A photograph is on an exposed negative, but it does not appear until the developer acts to bring it out—first faintly but finally in all its sharp contrast. The developer, however, has had no influence upon the content of the emerging picture. Or, children often shade a piece of paper placed over a coin. The structure of the coin determines the picture which emerges. No picture would have come out if the coin's surface had had no structure. But in addition, stroke after stroke of shading is necessary to bring out the underlying outline. Campaign propaganda has something like the effect of the developer and the pencil shading. It brings the voter's predispositions to the level of visibility and expression. It transforms the latent political tendency into a manifest vote.

The activating forces of political communications are of two types. First, there are the materials in the formal mass media—the newspaper, magazine, and radio. Secondly, there are direct personal influences which, as we shall see later, can be more important than widespread publicity, but that analysis must be reserved for another chapter. Here we shall be concerned mainly with the way in which the formal propaganda develops or activates the latent inclinations of the voter.

The Four Steps of Activation

There are four continuous steps in the normal process of activation. We shall state them here and then develop the evidence for each in more detail.

1. *Propaganda Arouses Interest:* As the campaign gains momentum, people who have not been interested begin to pay attention. At this stage it is the rising volume of propaganda which initiates the change.

2. *Increased Interest Brings Increased Exposure:* As people "wake up" to the campaign, their aroused attention leads them to see and hear more out of the supply around them. The

voter's initiative is more in evidence at this stage; but the relationship is circular. Increased attention brings increased exposure which further arouses interest and attention and adds to exposure and so on.

3. *Attention is Selective.* As interest increases and the voter begins to be aware of what it is all about, his predispositions come into play. Out of the wide array of available propaganda, he begins to select. He is more likely to tune in some programs than others; to go to some meetings rather than others; to understand one point in a speech than another. His selective attention thus reinforces the predispositions with which he comes to the campaign. At this stage the initiative is almost wholly with the prospective voter rather than with the propagandists. Whatever the publicity that is put out, it is the selective attention of the citizen which determines what is responded to.[2]

4. *Votes Crystallize.* Finally enough latent lines of thought and feeling have been aroused and sufficient rationale has been appropriated from the campaign so that the decision is made. The latent has become manifest; the uncertainty disappears; the voter is ready to mark his ballot.

Propaganda Arouses Attention

As more and more political propaganda poured into Erie County it broke over normal barriers of resistance and forced the election into everyone's attention. Some few, perhaps, remained impervious but for the county as a whole the developing campaign was accompanied by rising interest. Between May and October the proportion of respondents uninterested in the campaign fell from 13% to 7% and the proportion with a strong interest increased from 28% to 38% (Chart 26).

This general rise in interest might perhaps have been attributed merely to the approach of Election Day, were it not possible to study more closely the relationship between exposure to propaganda and the level of interest. The method will be explained here in some detail for it will be used several times in this study. Only on the basis of repeated interviews with the same individuals is it possible to analyze so carefully the relationship between influences abroad in the community and changes in opinion through time.

CHART 26
*Interest in the election invariably increases
as the campaign progresses.*

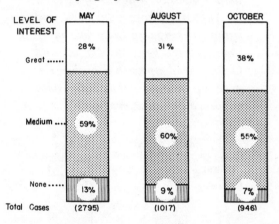

Let us start with the people who expressed a medium amount of interest in the campaign in August. We know how much political propaganda they read or listened to in the period between August and October as expressed in the general exposure index described in Chapter V. Now, let us divide the persons with medium interest into two groups—those with more than average exposure during that period and those with less. (A finer classification might be made but this has the advantages of simplicity and of keeping the number of cases sizeable.)

How did the interest level of these two groups change between August and October? All were on the medium interest level in August but by October some had gained and others had lost interest. And the amount of propaganda to which they were exposed did make a significant difference in interest (Chart 27). Of those with more than average exposure, 21% moved from medium interest to high whereas of those with less than

average exposure to propaganda, only 8% moved up from medium interest to high. It was not the passage of time alone
which accounted for the increase in interest, for time was con-

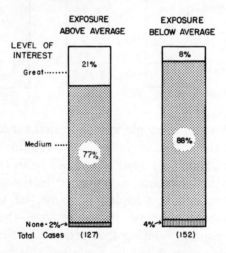

CHART 27

*This chart deals only with people
with a medium amount of interest
in August. Those who read and
listen to campaign materials more
than average between August and
October end up with a higher degree of interest than those with
exposure below average.*

stant for both groups. Nor can we account for the differences
in October by differences in initial level of interest for all were
alike (with some allowance for the broad steps of our scale) in
their medium concern with politics when the comparison began.
It was greater exposure during the August-October period
which resulted in a substantially greater interest level in October. (A similar comparison over an earlier and longer time
span—May to August—gave the same result.)

Increased Interest Brings Increased Exposure

Once interest has been aroused, the citizen begins to look for information on his own initiative. We have already seen, in Chapter V, that people with a greater interest in the election are also exposed in greater measure to the stream of propaganda. But can we show that it is the higher level of initial interest which brings about the greater exposure? Our repeated interviews make this possible. Again let us follow the method closely.

We shall start with pairs of groups which were alike in their exposure to political campaign materials during the May to August period. Two were high, two medium high, two medium low, and two low. In August one group in each pair reported a keen interest in the campaign; the other group lacked interest. The problem is: what happened to their exposure for the two paired groups, alike in their previous exposure but differing in interest?

During the August-October period, the more interested group in each pair read and listened more to campaign materials (Chart 28). The expected general tendency for the pairs with high exposure during May-August to continue relatively high during August-October is apparent from the slope of the whole chart. But we are concerned here with the differences *between* the bars in each pair. More interest in August meant more exposure to campaign materials during subsequent months.

This serves to demonstrate the second point in the activation process, that once interest has been aroused it operates to increase exposure. Actually, the two factors interact. The two results just described are part of a continuous process. Propaganda leads to increased interest which in turn makes people more willing to expose themselves to further propaganda, and so on.[3] But, as we shall see now, in the course of this process not all people are reached by the same kind of propaganda.

CHART 28

The four pairs of bars distinguish between people with different degrees of exposure in the first part of the campaign. They were divided according to their degree of interest in August. The more interested read and listened to more campaign material during the second part of the campaign, irrespective of their previous exposure level.

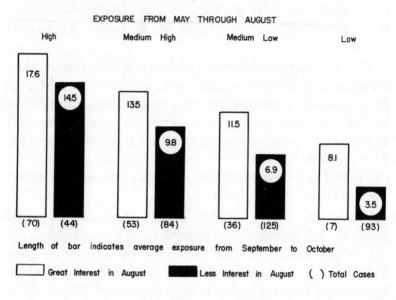

EXPOSURE FROM MAY THROUGH AUGUST

High   Medium High   Medium Low   Low

17.6
14.5
13.5
9.8
11.5
6.9
8.1
3.5

(70)   (44)   (53)   (84)   (36)   (125)   (7)   (93)

Length of bar indicates average exposure from September to October

☐ Great Interest in August   ■ Less Interest in August   ( ) Total Cases

Attention Is Selective

In a typical American presidential campaign, there is often not a complete balance between material favorable to the Democrats and that favorable to the Republicans, but still anyone who wants to read a particular side can usually find it. (The situation in Erie County in 1940 is described in Chapter XIII.) But supply need not be equated to exposure and actually was not. People selected political material in accord with their own taste and bias. Even those who had not yet made a decision exposed themselves to propaganda which fit their not-yet-conscious political predispositions.

This is easily demonstrated. The people who in August did not have a definite vote intention are classified by their index of political predispositions (IPP) into two groups: those with social characteristics which should predispose them to be Democrats and those with characteristics indicating Republican predispositions. Remember that these people had not yet made up their minds how they were going to vote. Next we look at their exposure to political communications but we do it differently from before. What interests us now is not the extent but *the political color* of the material to which they were exposed. All the speeches, magazine articles, or newspaper stories they reported reading or hearing were classified according to their political content. Thus we were able to classify the exposure of each respondent as predominantly Republican, predominantly Democratic, or neutral (the last if the respondent had neither heard nor read anything or if his attention was evenly balanced between the two parties).

The still-undecided persons with the economic, religious, and residential attributes which usually characterize Republicans managed as a rule to see and hear more Republican propaganda (Chart 29). Among those whose characteristics—economic, religious and residential—tended Democratic, three times as many saw and heard more pro-Democratic propaganda than pro-Republican.

There are at least two factors which account for the differences. One is external to the voter himself. He lives in the country so he reads farm journals that happen also to be more Republican; or he lives in the city so he hears more talk from fellow-workers who are pro-labor and pro-Democratic. The environment sifts the propaganda which the respondent sees and hears.

But there is also an effect caused by the still-unconscious psychological predispositions of the voter himself. From his many past experiences shared with others in his economic, religious, and community groups, he has a readiness to attend to some things more than others. His internal as well as his external situation is weighted one way or the other. Voters somehow contrive to select out of the passing stream of stimuli those by which they are more inclined to be persuaded. So it is that the more they read and listen, the more convinced they become of the rightness of their own position. And that brings us up to the final point—clinching the decision.

CHART 29

People who have not yet decided about their vote expose themselves more to propaganda of that party for which they are predisposed by background.

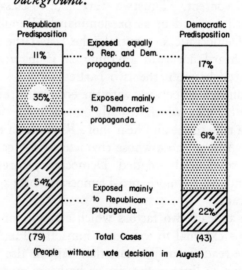

Republican Predisposition — Democratic Predisposition

11% ...... Exposed equally to Rep. and Dem. propaganda 17%

35% ...... Exposed mainly to Democratic propaganda 61%

54% ...... Exposed mainly to Republican propaganda 22%

(79)   Total Cases   (43)

(People without vote decision in August)

Votes Crystallize

The human being is biologically integrated for action. Thought and emotion may occasionally be nurtured for their own sake, but more frequently they are used to guide action. The normal outcome of the process of political activation is the act of voting. As we have seen, this is ordinarily reached in three stages: (1) the awareness of a campaign and the presence of propaganda warms up interest; (2) interest in turn sets off the quest for more information and creates the readiness to notice more of what has been available all the time; but (3) the voter's attention is steered by his predisposition, i.e., he discovers mainly what he will find acceptable. Political writers have the task of providing "rational" man with good and acceptable reasons to dress up the choice which is more effectively determined by underlying social affiliations. At some point along the line the evidence reaches a satisfactory level; the individual is persuaded; the choice is consciously completed.

In psychological terms the act of decision ends the internal competition. One system of values and loyalties — say, the Democratic—would, if put in operation, lead to one line of action. The other involves different (Republican) ways of looking at and feeling about the campaign. So long as the decision is withheld, both may be recognized as valid, and a few voters even shift from one framework to the other. But people are urged to vote and find it embarrassing to remain suspended between the sides and identified with neither. To decide means to discard what has been up to the time of decision a possible frame of thought and feeling and to act in accord with the other.

We have seen how the arguments read and heard by the respondents conform more and more to the outlook of their social groups. Arguments enter the final stage of decision more as *indicators* than as *influences*. They *point out*, like signboards along the road, the way to turn in order to reach a destination which is already determined. So, in a sense, it is for votes at this fourth stage. The political predispositions and group allegiances set the goal; all that is read and heard becomes helpful and effective insofar as it guides the voter toward his already "chosen" destination. The clinching argument thus does not have the function of *persuading* the voter to act. He furnishes the motive power himself. The argument has the function of *identifying* for him the way of thinking and acting which he is already half-aware of wanting. Campaigning for votes is not writing on a public *tabula resa;* it is showing men and women that their votes are a normal and logical and more or less inevitable expression of tendencies with which each has already aligned himself. Perhaps some illustrations may help to make clear all four stages of the process of activation.

Some Illustrations of Activation

The whole process of activation is rather complex and our respondents were not likely to be aware of it themselves. The following case is a typical example, from our interviews, of how the expression of political predispositions came about. This respondent is a Protestant store owner with an SES level of B, living in a rural part of the country. In the first months of the campaign period he could not decide which candidate he favored. He thought Roosevelt had been a good president, had instituted many important reforms, and had "kept us from the internal revolution that they said was threatening the country." He also stated that "if times were different, Willkie might be good." But his Republican predisposition naturally led him to propaganda favorable to the Republican party. And by September, constant reading of a newspaper which came out for Willkie had brought him into line with others of his social group: *"Now that he (Willkie) has come out and said what he was for*—defense is the most important thing—I plan to vote for him. . . . I also like his business program of trying not to interfere with business or burden business with taxes. *I have been reading the texts of Willkie's speeches* in the *Cleveland Plain Dealer."*

Another way to trace the role of activation is to see how the same argument takes different forms for respondents of differing backgrounds. One of the slogans in favor of Willkie was that he represented the American ideal of the poor boy who made good. The following three quotations illustrate how Willkie became all things to all men:

Well-to-do Railroad Foreman, Retired: "He is a *business*

man and that is what will most likely put the nation back on its feet. Roosevelt is all politician, and I wouldn't vote for anybody for a third term anyhow. . . ."

Poor Unemployed Musician: "Willkie is *for the poor people.* . . . I have been reading how he was a poor farmer boy and worked for 75 cents a day tending cows and how he was for the poor people. He has got to be president of some big company just through hard work. . . ."

Well-to-do Woman Engaged in Farming: "I am against the third term and since reading Willkie's life in the *Farm Journal* I am rather sure I will vote for him. I was waiting for both conventions before deciding. I am greatly impressed by an article in the *Farm Journal* that Willkie started as a poor boy and now owns *four farms* valued at $88,000."

It seems, incidentally, that the social function of such stereotypes can be better understood in the light of the internal and subjective selection of influences. A campaign argument will be particularly successful if a variety of meanings can be read into it. From this picture of the man who started humbly and became successful any of three different elements may be brought to the fore: the poor people can feel that he will not have forgotten them, the rich people can be convinced that he will take care of their interests, and the middle-class voters can be attracted by the implications of hard work and thrift which are so prominent in their own ideology. One may speak of structured and unstructured stereotypes. The former are too well defined to be useful. The unstructured are catch-alls into which each voter reads the meanings he desires.

A final example of activation can be taken from our own panel procedure. Interviewers returned to members of the panel six times and as a result, the interest of our panel members was increased. Their interest level became somewhat higher than that of the control group, and the panel members themselves testified to this effect. The proportion of the panel who actually voted was also somewhat higher than that of the county. But the *distribution* of votes was not affected by it. The interviewers activated the predispositions of some of our more sluggish respondents but did not affect the ratio in which they finally voted for the two parties.

Thus, personal relationships were also instrumental in activating the latent predispositions of the voters. Before dealing with them directly, however, let us turn to some other effects of the campaign.

CHAPTER IX

The Reinforcement Effect

Paradoxically enough, campaign propaganda exerted one major effect by producing no overt effect on vote behavior at all—if by the latter "effect" we naively mean a *change* in vote. Half the people knew in May, before the campaign got underway, how they would vote in November, and actually voted that way. But does that mean that campaign propaganda had no effect upon them? Not at all. For them, political communications served the important purpose of preserving prior decisions instead of initiating new decisions. It kept the partisans "in line" by reassuring them in their vote decision; it reduced defections from the ranks. It had the effect of reinforcing the original vote decision.

The importance of reinforcement can be appreciated by conjecturing what might have happened if the political content of the major media of communications had been monopolized, or nearly monopolized, by one of the parties. European experience with totalitarian control of communications suggests that under some conditions the opposition may be whittled down until only the firmly convinced die-hards remain. In many parts of this country, there are probably relatively few people who would tenaciously maintain their political views in the face of a continuous flow of hostile arguments. Most people want—and need—to be told that they are right and to know that other people agree with them. Thus, the parties could forego their propagandizing only at considerable risk, and never on a unilateral basis. So far as numbers of voters are concerned, campaign propaganda results not so much in gaining new adherents as in preventing the loss of voters already favorably inclined.

Wherever the parties stand in substantial competition—as they do throughout most of the country and as they did in Erie County in 1940—party loyalties are constantly open to the danger of corrosion. Party propaganda—from his own party— provides an arsenal of political arguments which serve to allay the partisan's doubts and to refute the opposition arguments which he encounters in his exposure to media and friends—in short, to secure and stabilize and solidify his vote intention and finally to translate it into an actual vote. A continuing flow of partisan arguments enables him to reinterpret otherwise unsettling events and counter-arguments so that they do not leave him in an uncomfortable state of mental indecision or inconsistency. For example, Republicans who might be disturbed by Willkie's relationship to utility interests were equipped with the notion that his experience in business would make him a better administrator of the national government than Roosevelt. Similarly, Democrats uneasy about the third term as a break with American tradition were able to justify it by reference to the President's indispensable experience in foreign affairs at such a time of world crisis. (In fact, this latter argument *was* the answer to the disturbing third-term argument for many loyal Democrats.)

The provision of new arguments and the reiteration of old arguments in behalf of his candidate reassure the partisan and strengthen his vote decision. Should he be tempted to vacillate, should he come to question the rightness of his decision, the reinforcing arguments are there to curb such tendencies toward defection. The partisan is assured that he is right; he is told why he is right; and he is reminded that other people agree with him, always a gratification and especially so during times of doubt. In short, political propaganda in the media of communication, by providing them with good partisan arguments, at the same time provides orientation, reassurance, integration for the already partisan. Such satisfactions tend to keep people "in line" by reinforcing their initial decision. To a large extent,

stability of political opinion is a function of exposure to reinforcing communications.

Partisanship, Partisan Exposure, Reinforced Partisanship

The availability of partisan propaganda in Erie County in
1940 was somewhat out of balance. There was much more
Republican material available (see Chapter XIII) but it was
still reasonably easy to read or listen to the Democratic side. If
the exposure of the partisans paralleled the partisan distribution
of available communications, they would always be running up
against the case of the opposition, especially the Democrats.
Thus reinforcement would take a step forward and then a step
back, and its effect would be halting and lame at best.

But, of course, actual exposure does *not* parallel availability.
Availability *plus* predispositions determines exposure—and predispositions lead people to select communications which are congenial, which support their previous position. More Republicans than Democrats listened to Willkie and more Democrats
than Republicans listened to Roosevelt. The universe of campaign communications — political speeches, newspaper stories,
newscasts, editorials, columns, magazine articles—was open to
virtually everyone. But exposure was consistently partisan, and
such partisan exposure resulted in reinforcement.[1]

By and large about two-thirds of the constant partisans—the
people who were either Republican or Democratic from May
right through to Election Day—managed to see and hear more
of their own side's propaganda than the opposition's.[2] About
one-fifth of them happened to expose more frequently to the
other side, and the rest were neutral in their exposure (Chart
30). But—and this is important—the more strongly partisan
the person, the more likely he is to insulate himself from contrary points of view. The constants with great interest and with
most concern in the election of their own candidate were *more*
partisan in exposure than the constants with less interest and less
concern. Such partisan exposure can only serve to reinforce the
partisan's previous attitudes. In short, the most partisan people

protect themselves from the disturbing experience presented by opposition arguments by paying little attention to them. Instead, they turn to that propaganda which reaffirms the validity and wisdom of their original decision—which is then reinforced.

CHART 30

The more interested people are in the election, the more they tend to expose themselves to propaganda of their own party. This chart deals only with those with constant vote intention from May to November.

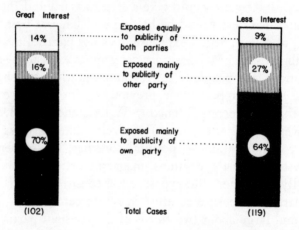

Great Interest		Less Interest
14%	Exposed equally to publicity of both parties	9%
16%	Exposed mainly to publicity of other party	27%
70%	Exposed mainly to publicity of own party	64%
(102)	Total Cases	(119)

One of the assumptions of a two-party democratic system is that considerable inter-communication goes on between the supporters of the opposing sides. This evidence indicates that such inter-communication may go on in public—in the media of communication—without reaching very far into the ranks of the strongly partisan, on either side. In recent years, there has been a good deal of talk by men of good will about the desirability and necessity of guaranteeing the free exchange of ideas in the market-place of public opinion. Such talk has centered upon the problem of keeping free the channels of expression and communication. Now we find that the consumers of ideas, if they have made a decision on the issue, themselves erect high tariff walls against alien notions.

Reinforcement Described by the Reinforced

Partisans need reasons for being partisan, and the formal media supply them and thus reinforce their partisanship. At one point during the interviews, the respondents who maintained a constant voting preference were asked why they favored the candidate of their choice. Their answers sometimes showed the effect of reinforcement.

Faint beginnings of doubt about the wisdom of their decision were counteracted by appropriate propaganda, and corrosion is thus halted. For example, a young married woman, a Democrat with low income, reported: "In FDR's Wednesday night speech, he stated the facts of his administration. He mentioned several facts of which I had been unaware—for example, that there have been fewer bank failures in his administration than in previous ones. I cannot recall any others at present, but *I had no idea FDR had accomplished so much.*" The final phrase clearly expresses this partisan's relief and gratification in the apparent validity of her decision.

Similar reinforcement—the other side of the coin—is evident in the case of a young salesman on a low SES level who was for Willkie in 1940 just as he had been for Landon in 1936. His actual economic position conflicted with his appraisal of himself as belonging to small business. He granted that "Roosevelt's policies were good but we don't need them now," and then continued: "I have been reading various articles about Roosevelt lately and he didn't do as much as I thought. . . . Read in *Nation's Business* about the NLRB. The basic idea was all right but they didn't push it far enough. *It just sounds like he has done a lot but he really didn't.*" This man's wife disagreed with him on politics. Under all these cross-pressures, perhaps insecure in his Republican vote intention, he turned to business publications to reassure himself, to convince himself that he was right, and to get good ideas for purposes of argument. Without such reinforcement, this man might have swung away from the Republicans.

But some respondents had more than the faint beginnings of doubt; they had enough doubts actually to leave their original choice for indecision or even the other party, after which they returned to their first decision. Such people are the waverers we have discussed in earlier chapters. The influence exerted upon them by the media of communication to return to their original decision is no less a reinforcement effect than that exerted upon someone who doubted but never actually left his party. It is just that they needed *more* reinforcement.

Consider the case of a young unemployed laborer on a low SES level—a "natural" Democrat. Originally Democratic, he favored Roosevelt because "he gave us work" and because he is "damned if he knows" who will benefit from Willkie's election. And yet he decided in August to vote Republican because of the third term issue: "Two times is enough. The rest of 'em didn't take it." But then he heard an argument which served to reinforce his Democratic predispositions: "I heard a Lowell Thomas broadcast yesterday saying that *Hitler and Mussolini wanted Willkie elected.* I don't want to vote for any Bund." And so this respondent returned to his Democratic vote intention because "FDR has the experience we need at this time and I don't have the confidence in Willkie, without experience in this crisis." And once again, he cited his favorite commentator, Lowell Thomas, as the source of this reason for change.

Another illustration of the effect of reinforcement upon a waverer involves the vice-president of a bank, with strong Republican predispositions. In May he was Republican, but by June—after Germany's conquest of Western Europe—he was not sure: "My decision will depend upon who will keep us out of war. That is paramount in my mind." But all his attitudes and values, and probably associates, were so firmly Republican that his indecision was short-lived. By August he was back doing business at the same old stand: "For one thing, FDR's running for a third term made me very disgusted ... *Any man*

(*Willkie*) *who has made such a success of himself in such a big business* as Commonwealth and Southern will do a lot for this country in a business way. I've read articles about him in the *Cleveland Plain Dealer* and also the *Chicago Tribune*. I have also read a book, 'The Smoke Screen,' which woke me up to just how badly FDR is spending the taxpayers' money."

It is in comments of this kind that we find indications of the reinforcement functions of partisan arguments. They reinforce by validating, orienting, and strengthening the original decision, by minimizing tendencies toward an internal conflict of opinions, by buttressing some opinions at the expense of others, and by countering possible or actual corrosion of partisan attitudes.

CHAPTER X

The Conversion Effect

Campaign propaganda activated people by bringing their latent political attitudes to the surface of recognition and expression. It reinforced people by telling them what they most wanted to see and hear. But what of the third effect of campaign propaganda—conversion? When people speak of the influence of the press and radio, that is usually what they mean. Were people actually convinced by campaign propaganda to renounce their original choice in favor of the opposition or to decide upon a vote contrary to that ordinarily associated with their social characteristics? How often did conversion occur and how did it work?

The first thing to say is that some people *were* converted by campaign propaganda but that they were *few indeed.* What we have already learned about the factors involved in vote decisions makes this less than surprising. Clearly, several factors other than short-run communications took precedence in influence. Such factors or conditions actually served to insulate various groups from the conversion influence, thus delimiting its area of application. In combination, they acted as a fine political sieve through which relatively few people passed. As the following summary briefly indicates, a whole set of established behavior patterns operated against conversion and hence made it an uncommon experience.

Restriction 1: Half the people knew in May for which party they would vote and clung to this choice throughout the campaign. They were the least susceptible to conversion.

Restriction 2: Of those who were undecided in May, about

half made up their minds after they knew who the nominees were and maintained this decision throughout the campaign. Such partisans, who made their choice conditional on the nominee, were likewise not open to ready conversion.

Restriction 3: The vote decisions of 70% of the people, whether or not they expressed an early vote intention, corresponded to the vote tendencies prevailing among groups with social characteristics similar to their own. The predispositions of such people were so deeply rooted that they could not be readily converted by the opposition's campaign propaganda.

Restriction 4: The strongly partisan devoted most attention to campaign propaganda. In other words, the people who read and listened most to political communications had the most fixed political views. Thus, in sheer quantity campaign propaganda reached the persons least amenable to conversion.[1]

Restriction 5: The people who read and heard most political communication were exposed to more of their own partisan propaganda. Thus in partisanship too, attention to propaganda led away from conversion.[2]

In summary, then, the people who did most of the reading and listening not only read and heard most of their own partisan propaganda but were also most resistant to conversion because of their strong predispositions. And the people who were most open to conversion—the ones the campaign managers most wanted to reach—read and listened least. Those inter-related facts represent the bottleneck of conversion.

But although these restrictions considerably narrow the application of conversion, they do not eliminate it altogether. For the sake of the record, let us definitely establish the occurrence of conversion on the basis of campaign communications available in the formal media. To do so, we must show that exposure to partisan propaganda leads some people to vote against their predispositions. Within the limitations outlined above, this does happen (Chart 31). Persons with Republican predispositions who were exposed to predominantly Democratic propaganda voted more Democratic than those with the same predisposi-

CHART 31

Exposure to political propaganda has a converting effect: people predisposed toward the Republicans vote more Democratic if they are exposed to Democratic propaganda. The same finding holds for those with Democratic predispositions.

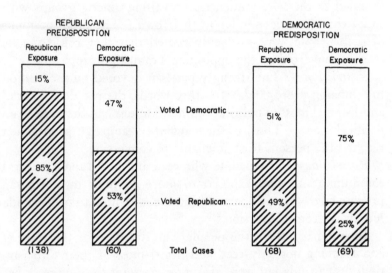

tions who were exposed to predominantly Republican propaganda. And the same was true for those with Democratic predispositions. Among people with definite predispositions, then, a certain proportion exposed to propaganda in opposition to their predisposition voted *in line with the propaganda* and *out of line with their predispositions.* Such people were converted by campaign propaganda.

The Conversion Effect Illustrated—The Third Term Issue

Every campaign has its major issues and arguments which are supposed to be not only the most "important" but also the most effective in converting voters. In 1940, the major Republican argument—perhaps the major issue of the whole campaign—

was the third term. What success did it have in converting people?

Naturally, almost all the Republicans disapproved of the third term in principle, and most of the Democrats favored it. But this indicates nothing as to its value as a converting argument. To show how influential for conversion it "really" was, we must set up rigid criteria. Let us say that the third term issue *could have* converted to a 1940 Republican vote only those who (1) voted for Roosevelt in 1936 *and* (2) did not intend to vote Republican in May, 1940 (i.e., before Roosevelt was nominated) *and* (3) believed that Roosevelt had been a good president. The application of these criteria narrows the field considerably, but at the same time it serves to delimit sharply the "real" converting influence exerted by the argument. If we find that such people ascribed their Republican vote in 1940 to the third term issue, then we may agree that it exerted a "real" influence upon them.

Of all the persons who changed toward Willkie during the course of the campaign, only 15 qualified on all these criteria of good-will toward Democratic policies. Of those, only nine mentioned the third term as the most important reason for their final vote decision when queried just after Election Day. But only six of them gave the third term as the *sole* reason for change at the time they shifted to a Republican position. According to our criteria, then, the third term issue served as a "real" converting influence only for these few people—about 2% of the total Republican vote. (And even then, probably not all six were "real" converts, since five of them had mixed political predispositions tending toward Republican. Thus, even the 2% for whom the third term argument was "really" effective were partly activated and only partly converted to a Republican vote.)

One clear case of the effectiveness of the third term argument—the one clear case as outlined above—is presented by a poor Catholic carpenter on the lowest SES level, obviously a man with strong Democratic predispositions. He had voted for

Roosevelt in 1932 and 1936 (and for Al Smith in 1928), he approved what Roosevelt had accomplished, and he originally had planned to vote for him again—but "the third term is a stumbling block." When he finally decided to vote Republican in August, he explained his change in these terms: "I have changed because of the third term. *I don't approve FDR's running for a third term.* He wants to be the first dictator in the United States. . . . *This will be the first time I have ever voted for a Republican.* I am voting for Willkie despite the fact that he's talking too much and making too many promises he won't be able to fulfill."

Thus, insofar as mass media of communications led to conversion at all, it was through a redefinition of the issues. In this example and others, issues about which people had previously thought very little or had been little concerned, took on a new importance as they were accented by campaign propaganda. In this way, political communications occasionally broke down traditional party loyalties.

Willkie, Champion of the Poor

The third term issue was a "natural" for the Republicans. But one propaganda problem which faced them was to convince voters on the low SES strata that Willkie had their interests at heart. The Republican pro-business tradition as well as Willkie's utility background worked against him in this regard.

In all, there were 14 people on the lowest SES level who changed to Willkie for economic reasons. These respondents were deviates from the general trend, which would suggest that they were converted by what they read and heard. Republican propagandists were successful in twisting the Democratic argument that "Willkie is in league with big business" into a form which would appeal most to these low-income people. It is interesting that a few of the respondents specifically mention Gerald L. K. Smith or Townsend as the sources of their opinions. Their reasoning follows these lines: "Willkie promised work, and *the Republican party is the money party so he will be able to keep his promise"*; "Willkie would increase wages because *he was born poor. Roosevelt was born wealthy* and doesn't know what it was like to be poor"; "Willkie will throw out New Deal measures. *Cooperating with capital will create work."*

The "Doubters"

Finally, there was a small number of conversion cases—very small—who were greatly interested in the election, who felt that there was something important to be said for each side, who tried more or less conscientiously to resolve their doubts one way or the other during the campaign. They, and only they, conformed to the standard stereotype of the dispassionate, rational democratic voter.

For the most part, such persons had "weak" predispositions, i.e., they tended to fall at or near the center of the IPP score. In other words, their social position was such that they could "afford" conversion through thought. Such people had established for themselves certain criteria by which to judge a presidential candidate—criteria formulated in terms of the interests of the country as a whole rather than the interests of a special group—but they were in doubt as to whether Roosevelt or Willkie fit the specifications better. They were subject to strong attitudinal cross-pressures (resulting from their "weak" predispositions); they liked Roosevelt for this and Willkie for that, or they approved one part of a candidate's program but disapproved another part. They gave some evidence of careful and objective thought about the problem of casting their ballot.

For example, here is a young man with slightly Republican predispositions. This first voter—rated extremely fair-minded by the interviewer—had a high school education and a little better than average means. He considered experience in business and in government equally important in a president, approved conscription but with reservations, was not particularly impressed by the third-term argument, and thought Willkie and Roosevelt agreed on most issues. He approved Roosevelt because "he has handled the problems of the middle class very well" and he liked Willkie because of his business and executive ability. He was undecided in vote until the last few days of the campaign and then settled on Roosevelt. Said he:

"I would rather have the man with the practical experience than the untried man. The two men seemed to think along the same lines and be on the same platform and it seemed that about the only difference was that one was experienced and the other was not. Willkie is a smart man in his line but he is not qualified to be president now because of the European situation. If the Republicans had put up a man like Taft, I might have voted Republican. No new information has come up to help form my opinion. It was just that I wanted to weigh facts right up to the end and keep my mind open to new information. . . ."

The real doubters—the open-minded voters who make a sincere attempt to weigh the issues and the candidates dispassionately for the good of the country as a whole—exist mainly in deferential campaign propaganda, in textbooks on civics, in the movies, and in the minds of some political idealists. In real life, they are few indeed.

CHAPTER XI

The Over-All Effect of
the Campaign

The presidential campaign as a whole, then—the speeches, the events, the writings, the discussions, the total propaganda output—had three effects upon the voters. The campaign activated the indifferent, reinforced the partisan, and converted the doubtful. We have suggested the relative importance of these effects of the campaign. Let us now summarize by a somewhat more systematic approach to the problem of the over-all effect of the campaign.

November 1936-to-May 1940 as Against May-to-October 1940

The proper perspective on a presidential campaign is gained only by a consideration of the changes from one presidential election to another. Only then can one basic question be answered: does the formal campaign during the summer and fall of an election year simply extend the long-term voting trend evident from election to election? Or does the campaign hasten or retard the trend line? In other words, what does the campaign do that would not have been done by the mere passage of time?

This problem is part of the problem of voting cycles. Presidential elections since the Civil War have moved in long-time trends from one party to the other.[1] From a low of 35% of the two-party vote in 1924, the Democrats reached a peak of 62% in 1936. Between 1936 and 1940, the Democratic majority fell off, but remained a majority. How much of such gross change occurs *between* one election and the beginning of the next campaign and how much occurs *during* the campaign?

In Erie County in 1940, changes in vote intention *during* the campaign were much fewer than changes in vote intention during the preceding three-and-a-half years. Everybody who stayed with the Republicans in 1936, a lean year, was also Republican in 1940 (actually, 99%). But the abnormally heavy Democratic vote in 1936 diminished as time went on. Between Election Day, 1936, and May, 1940, 21% of the 1936 Democrats had fallen away from the party. Between May and October, 1940, only another 8% left the Democratic fold. In other words, all the events of the intermediate period—local, national and international—changed over twice as many votes as all the events of the campaign.

What the campaign did was to speed up the long-term trend toward the Republicans. The 8% change during the six months of the campaign represents a greater change per unit of time than the 21% change during the 42 intervening months. The campaign served not only to extend the trend but to intensify it. The movement away from the Democrats from 1936 to 1940, so to speak, was activated by the whole business of the campaign.

TABLE V: THE EFFECT OF THE CAMPAIGN UPON VOTE INTENTIONS (MAY TO OCTOBER)

VOTE INTENTION IN MAY	VOTE INTENTION IN OCTOBER		
	VOTE INTENTION FOLLOWED PREDISPOSITIONS	VOTE INTENTION RAN COUNTER TO PREDISPOSITIONS	UNDECIDED
Vote Intention Followed Predispositions	Reinforcement 36%	Conversion 2%	Partial Conversion 3%
Vote Intention Ran Counter to Predispositions	Reconversion 3%	Reinforcement 17%	Partial Conversion 3%
Undecided	Activation 14%	Conversion 6%	No effect 16%

Assessment of Campaign Effects

That sets the stage for the following summary of the three effects of the campaign—activation, reinforcement, conversion. (The same effects of political communications, of course, operated between elections as well.)

The three effects were defined as they were discussed. For purposes of clarity and summary, let us represent them and the numbers of people to whom they apply in a single table (Table V). The table covers all the possible vote combinations at two different times. The data apply only to the status of vote intentions as of May and October; obviously, many changes went on *between* these two points in time and they could be run out similarly. But the May-October relationship, from beginning to end of the campaign, is the best single illustration of the basic matter—the nature and extent of campaign effects. In sum, then, this is what the campaign does: reinforcement (potential) 53%; activation 14%; reconversion 3%; partial conversion 6%; conversion 8%; no effect 16%.

But a few important caveats must be entered. We cannot say for sure whether all the constants were really reinforced by the campaign; certainly not all of them *needed* reinforcement. But no other effect than reinforcement could have operated for them. In this case, the figure certainly represents the maximum application of the effect. The same is true in the case of conversion, but for another reason. The data are based upon a relatively rough designation of predispositions, the IPP constructed in Chapter III and involving only the three primary characteristics of SES level, religion, and residence. A finer index of predispositions, containing basic political attitudes as well as additional such personal characteristics, would provide a much more reliable result—and would probably lower the figure for actual conversion. For example, many cases listed under conversion here refer to persons with relatively "weak" predispositions, i.e., persons with cross-pressures acting upon their vote decisions. A more exact measure of their original predispositions would undoubtedly eliminate a good many of them from the ranks of the converted.

And, to follow this up, those eliminated would enter the ranks of the activated, i.e., they would have made their vote decision in line with their actual political predispositions. In short, the figure for activation is probably low and the figure for conversion is probably high.[2] In any case conversion is, by far, the least frequent result and activation the second most frequent manifest effect of the campaign.

CHAPTER XII

Anticipation of the Winner

During a presidential campaign, most people know how they are going to vote and think they know who is going to win the election. In the following chapter, we shall see that a large proportion of the communications on the campaign is given over to just such speculation and prediction. Do editors and commentators meet a public need by playing up the contest element in the election?

In order to study this matter we asked our respondents the following question at every interview: "Regardless of which man or party you would like to see elected, which party do you think actually will be elected?"

Although the respondents were always Republican in the majority, they always expected the Democrats to win. Among those who had a definite expectation as to who would win, the proportion of those who favored Willkie was at its lowest in June just prior to the Republican convention and when the war situation in Europe was most exciting; at that time only 29% thought the Republicans would win. After the Republican convention came a sudden increase in those favoring the Republicans. From the Democratic convention on, the proportion of those who gave the Republicans the better chance varied between 46% and 48%.

The number of people who had no vote intention diminished gradually as the campaign progressed, but the figures show a different trend for expectation of winner. Up to the nominations, one-third did not express an opinion on who would win. After both candidates were known, the proportion of people without a definite expectation dropped to one-fourth and stayed there.

Expectations were considerably more uncertain than vote intention. While 48% never changed the party for which they intended to vote, only 25% kept the same expectation as to who would win the election all through the campaign. The more interested people were, the less did they change their expectation. For every ten people who throughout the study thought that the same candidate had the best chance, there were fifteen on the high interest level who changed their minds, 24 on the middle interest level, and 30 on the lowest.

As could be expected, there was a close relationship between vote intention and expectation of winner. By and large each party expected its own candidate to win and the people who had no vote intention were also not interested enough to form much of an opinion as to the probable winner.

The greater the interest in the election, the closer the relationship between expectation and vote intention. For people on the highest interest level the two factors have a Pearson correlation of .68; for those on the lower levels combined the correlation is only .59.[1]

Changes in Expectation

Whenever a respondent changed his expectation between two interviews, he was asked what made him change his mind. An analysis of the comments of these respondents aptly illustrates the importance of personal contacts. When people explained their changes in vote *intention*, they gave as sources of their decision radio or newspaper or personal conversations with other people in about the same frequency. But when they named their reasons for change in *expectation*, they mentioned face-to-face contacts with other people slightly more frequently than both formal media taken together.

There seemed to be two main ways in which people influenced each other's expectations. First, someone can be told by someone else that the chances of a candidate have changed, as exemplified in the following quotation from the interviews:

"*People say* each time Willkie speaks he loses a lot of votes. I don't know myself but I believe he may lose out."

Secondly, the respondent formed his own conclusions by watching what went on around him. He did not need to be told because he could see the signs on the wall himself:

"On previous interviews it seemed as though more people were for Roosevelt. But the third term is against him, *the people don't like* the way he made the trade with England for the naval bases without conferring with Congress, so now I am not so sure any more who will win."

It is interesting to observe that as the campaign progressed the former kind of remark—where our respondents just took over other people's predictions—decreased and the latter kind of comment—where our respondents observed what other people felt—increased until in October the two kinds of comments were about equally frequent.

The reading of our material gives a very strong impression that in political discussions the question of who will win is the most frequent topic among people, although our data are not set up to permit a definite statement on this point.

The Bandwagon Effect

This leads directly to a basic question: was there a bandwagon effect? The answer is yes. The respondents who had not formed a vote intention in May can be classified by the candidate they expected to win. In October some of these people had decided which candidate they wanted to support. The subsequent vote intention followed the preceding expectation (Chart 32).

In everyone of twenty-one such charts which can be formed from our material by comparing interviews taken at different times, the same result was obtained.[2]

The influence of expectation on vote intention is psychologically a rather complicated one. Probably some people had already half made up their minds for whom to vote but it seemed less dangerous to put it in the form of an expectation rather than vote intention. In other cases, hearing about a candidate's chances might have activated a predisposition already existing. But in some cases, respondents did not hesitate to say straight out that they were deliberately trying to vote for the winner:

"Just before the election it looked like Roosevelt would win so I went with the crowd. Didn't make any difference to me who won, but *I wanted to vote for the winner*."

"I have always been a Democrat, but lately I've heard of so many Democrats who are going to vote Republican that *I might do the same*. Four out of five Democrats I know are doing that."

CHART 32

People tend to vote for the candidate they expect to win.

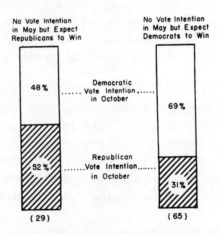

Undoubtedly, then, a bandwagon effect does exist and campaign managers do well to take full advantage of it. There are undeniably people for whom direct argumentation would be less effective than the impression that everyone is supporting one candidate. There were many ways to influence people's expectations as to the winner. We repeatedly found references of the following kind:

"I have heard *a number of Democrats* on radio voting for Willkie—Irvin Cobb, John L. Lewis. I therefore feel that Willkie will get it, with such backing."

"I heard over the radio the other night that one of the *largest betting houses in New York* was betting 9 to 5 on Roosevelt and when they give those odds, there is really something to it. Also heard a broadcast from Hollywood where *leading movie stars* are coming out for Roosevelt."

Public opinion polls as a source of change in expectation were explicitly mentioned by forty-two respondents.[3]

CHAPTER XIII

What the Voters Were Told

To the people of Erie County, as to the people of the United States at large, the presidential campaign of 1940 was brought home in the available communications—newspapers, magazines, radio newscasts, speeches, pamphlets, personal conversations. What appeared in these sources represented the campaign for the voters. What were the people told?[1]

This report is based upon an analysis of important campaign communications coming into Erie County through the most widely read newspapers and magazines and through the most listened-to speeches and newscasts.[2] Actually, the magazine stories and the radio speeches were nation-wide in coverage, and so duplicated the appearance of the campaign available most other places throughout the country. The same is true, though to a lesser extent, of the newspaper accounts of the campaign, which were usually the accounts available from the major wire services. The newspaper columnists available in Erie County also appeared in newspapers throughout the United States. In short, the following account of the appearance of the campaign to the reader and listener in Erie County would probably not vary much for the reader and listener in many places throughout the country.

Three samples were chosen at different stages of the campaign. The first, August 5 to 10, came during the pre-campaign lull between the Democratic convention and Willkie's acceptance speech which started the actual campaigning, at least for the Republicans. The second period, October 12 to 17, catches the increasing tempo of the campaign at the start of the final month, just after Willkie's tour of the East and coinciding with the President's "non-political" inspection of defense plants (in which he made speeches at Akron and Dayton in Ohio). The third and final period, October 25 to November 4, covered the last and most active eleven days of the campaign.

Partisanship: How Much Supported Whom?

The most interesting single question about the content of communications on the campaign is this: to what extent did they support one candidate as against the other? The answer is that the Republican position was presented just over twice as heavily as the Democratic position, in all the public communications readily available in Erie County (Table VI).

TABLE VI: PARTISANSHIP: TIME PERIODS

	August 5-10	Oct. 12-17	Oct. 25-Nov 4	Total	
Republican	49%	63%	52%	55%	
Pro-Willkie	29	23	19		21
Anti-Roosevelt	20	40	33		34
Democratic	15	20	29	25	
Pro-Roosevelt	8	11	17		14
Anti-Willkie	7	9	12		11
Neutral	36	17	19	20	

During the earliest period, just before Willkie's acceptance speech, his partisans devoted themselves to building him up but by the time the campaign reached the homestretch their efforts were largely directed to attacks on Roosevelt. As for the Democrats, they centered their propaganda increasingly upon their own candidate. Balanced and neutral statements, which made up over one-third of the campaign discussions in early August, were cut in half during the crucial verbal battle of the last month.

What of the communication media themselves? How did they reflect the campaign, in terms of straight partisanship? (Table VII). As a whole, the magazines were most partisan (3 to 1), the newspapers next (just over 2 to 1), and the radio broadcasts least (just under 2 to 1). This calls for some discussion.

TABLE VII: PARTISANSHIP: MEDIA OF COMMUNICATION

	Newspaper	Radio	Magazine
Republican	54%	54%	58%
Pro-Willkie	18	17	34
Anti-Roosevelt	36	37	24
Democratic	26	29	19
Pro-Roosevelt	15	16	10
Anti-Willkie	11	13	9
Neutral	20	17	23

The term "partisanship" is used here in a strictly objective sense, simply to denote the support of one or the other side. No connotation of deliberate distortion is implied. However, this question is crucial to the problem of democratic communication. Unless partisans on all sides of a controversial issue believe that the media of communication provide them with a reasonably fair picture of the controversy, their faith in the media turns to suspicion and then to outright disbelief, and as a result political groups may come to lack any common ground for public discussion. (Some evidence for this is presented in Chapter XIV).

The partisanship of printed media, for the Republicans particularly, has been much discussed in recent years and is therefore not a surprising result. That the content of radio time has almost the same character is to be explained by two factors. For one, it appears that within the period sampled, Republican speakers bought much more time on the air than did the Democrats. (A more specific analysis shows that the difference was considerably smaller in the last few weeks before the election, when Roosevelt went on the air himself.) But in addition, the preponderance of Republican speakers also influenced the political color of the radio newscasts themselves. After all, if the Republican campaign is a more vigorous one, the newscasters have to report more Republican speeches. It is useful to distinguish between the direct and the reflected political content of radio time during the campaign. The direct content, composed of partisan speeches, had this composition in our sample: 58% Republican, 29% Democratic, and 13% neutral. For the reflected content, composed of newscasts, the distribution was as follows: 46% Republican, 27% Democratic, and 27% neutral. The newscasts were more balanced than the partisan speakers.

This can be documented by reference to the partisanship of the three Sandusky newspapers in the 1940 presidential campaign. One of the papers was strongly Republican, another was traditionally (and less strongly) Democratic, and the third was nominally Democratic but actually neutral. The gross partisanship of the three papers differed (Table VIII). Now all three papers were reporting to their readers the same external events —the events of the campaign—for the same time periods. If the papers were strictly objective in their reporting, the readers of all three would have been given roughly the same picture of the campaign, in terms of over-all partisanship. Actually, however, they were not. The Republican paper managed to stress the Republican side, the Democratic paper managed to stress the Democratic side, and the neutral paper—undoubtedly more reliable than either of the others in simply *reflecting* the campaign—managed to strike a balance between the other two.

TABLE VIII: PARTISANSHIP: THREE LOCAL PAPERS

	Republican Paper	Neutral Paper	Democratic Paper
Pro-Republican	72%	54%	46%
Pro-Democratic	14	17	36
Neutral	14	29	18

This distribution, in fact, illustrates *both* the reflection of and the selection from the campaign, i.e., the effects of both reportage and partiality. The Republicans campaigned longer and hence made more reportable news, and this is evident in the partisanship of all three papers—even the Democratic paper, which was thus "forced" by events to give somewhat more weight to the opposing candidate. Within this framework, however, the papers did what they could to express their own editorial policies, and the figures on partisanship show how successful they were. Perhaps the distance between the neutral paper and each of the others can be taken as a measure of the relative emphasis of the reporting function as against the partisan function, in this situation.

The particular slant taken by the magazines tells a story of its own. The magazines alone were strongly pro-Willkie; the emphasis on the Republican side both in radio and newspaper was almost as strongly anti-Roosevelt. This pro-Willkie material consisted largely of biographies and sketches of the candidate and was hence a "natural" for the American mass magazine. Such life stories and character delineations constitute one standard ingredient in the make-up of American magazines. The careers and personalities of "interesting" people of the day are always being described in such magazines, and Willkie's story fitted this formula perfectly. It was a typical American success story of the man suddenly placed in the center of the public stage, and the magazines played their specialty heavily. (Roosevelt was too familiar a figure for such treatment, and he got little of it.) Of course, at the same time the editors felt that they were both satisfying their readers' expectations and fulfilling the need to acquaint them with this relatively unknown politician. Whatever the motivation—whether inspired by public or private reasons—the fact remains that the magazines, relatively free from the compulsions to reflect the news, were strongly Republican and within that were strongly pro-Willkie rather than anti-Roosevelt.

All of this documents the commonplace notion that the essence of a presidential campaign is partisanship, but just *how* partisan is it? An answer can be found by ascertaining the amount of neutral statements and of admissions in stories and speeches which clearly supported one or the other candidate. Only those items are included here which openly favored one side, e.g., partisan speeches and statements, flattering character sketches, partisan argumentation by columnists, etc. If an item as a whole was neutral or balanced, it was omitted from consideration here. Of all the material in such clearly partisan items, nearly 80% favored the candidate supported by the item as a whole. Another 15% were neutral, and only about 5% conceded some virtue to the other side. Whether the American public, or that part of it not itself strongly partisan, sees in such extreme one-sidedness a distortion of reality is problematic. More likely, such partisanship is either attributed to the usual behavior of "politicians" or interpreted within the framework of American sport where the main objective is to win. For better or for worse, the presidential campaign is depicted almost exclusively in black or white.

Subject-Matter: Main Emphases and Themes

Within this most general framework of partisanship, what topics did campaign propaganda deal with? What subjects were the people told most about?

The most talked-about subject matter during the campaign was the campaign itself. Over a third of all discussion centered on the progress of the campaign, on the campaign methods of the two parties, and particularly on speculations about the candidates' chances. Next came the Roosevelt record, with another one-fourth of the campaign material devoted to it. These topics were followed by the future policies of Willkie and Roosevelt and by discussions of the candidates themselves.

The appearance of the election as a contest in which opponents struggle for the advantage derives in part from the emphasis on prognoses dealing with the campaign. On the one hand, the protagonists and their supporters sought to create the illusion of victory-already-won; and on the other hand, the independent commentators sought to establish themselves as shrewd analysts of the progress of the campaign. As a result, the outcome of the election received considerable attention. The developing campaign was discussed and predicted at every stage, just as sports writers speculate about the outcome of the World Series or next Saturday's football game. To some extent, this is a clue to the strong feelings on the part of the constant partisans: they wanted their team to win.

In the 1940 campaign, in the nature of the case, the President stood on his record whereas Willkie had to sell himself as a "future." As a result, the battle of the "issues" was a battle between Roosevelt's record and Willkie's promises.

An administration's record, simply as a history of something tangible done or left undone, is always open to criticism from those whose function it is to recommend other ways of doing the same things. Campaign promises, on the other hand, are easily made by everyone. In a presidential campaign, each side takes pains to draw its own attractive blueprints of the future rather than concentrate on pointing out the flaw in the opponents' and thus focus public attention on them. This general proposition was borne out in the 1940 election propaganda. Each side attacked its opponents' record more than that record was defended. And, to an even greater degree, each side spent more time in advocating its own future policies than in objecting to its opponents'. When the record was being discussed, attack predominated over defense by about 3 to 2. When future policy was being discussed, praise predominated over attack by about 2 to 1. In short, "their side" made the most mistakes and "our side" makes the best promises.

Although the 1940 campaign began just after the fall of France and ended just after the Axis attack in the Balkans, the foreign situation took a back seat to domestic problems in campaign propaganda. Of the total discussion of the issues, 73% dealt with domestic issues and only 27% with foreign affairs. In the light of subsequent events, this distribution of attention may seem out of proportion to the relative importance of the two topics.

The unprecedented "challenge to American traditions" in 1940 made the third term a natural talking point—for the Republicans. Fully 85% of all references to the third term were opposed to it. In addition, the Democrats argued specifically for the third term as such less than for any other subject; of some 1,200 pro-Roosevelt sentences only 13 were *overtly* pro-third term. The Democrats were content to handle the question by avoiding it, lest they simply add fuel to the Republican fire. Furthermore there was less neutral discussion of it than of any other topic (7% as against an average of 20%).

The Center of the Campaign: Roosevelt

There is a political legend in the United States that presidential campaigns are waged, and presidential elections decided, for and against *one* of the candidates rather than for both of them. Thus the campaign of 1928 is said to have been settled on a pro- or anti-Al Smith basis. In 1932 the central figure was supposed to be Hoover and in 1936 Roosevelt. Whatever the extent to which this legend is borne out in these and earlier elections, there is some evidence on the situation in 1940, at least so far as the campaign propaganda is concerned.

First, however, one caution against generalization. If any recent campaign *should* support the legend it would be the campaign of 1940, in which the President for two historic terms was standing for re-election on his much-debated record. His opponent, a newcomer to politics with no record of his own to stand on, was virtually forced to define his position by reference to the incumbent's administration. Thus the circumstances of the election stacked the deck in favor of the legend— as of course they may for every election.

The campaign material in press and radio *favored* Willkie slightly more than 2-to-1, but it *centered* on Roosevelt 3-to-2. Thus *partisanship* and *focus* are far from identical. Both the material favoring the Republicans and that favoring the Democrats dealt with the President more than with his opponent. In other words, the former was more anti-Roosevelt than pro-Willkie and the latter was more pro-Roosevelt than anti-Willkie (see Table VI).

The Ends of the Campaign: History, Money, Security

The major end of a political campaign is to win the election. In order to do this, however, the candidate must offer the voter some inducement to gain his vote. As is evident above, most campaign propaganda consisted of an attempt to show that "our policies" are good and "their policies" are bad. But what were the policies supposed to be good or bad *for?* What were the (future) goals and (past) results in terms of which policies, plans, decisions, beliefs, acts were justified? What was the voter to get for his vote? The answer suggests which appeals the candidates and their managers thought most effective for American voters.

The major social goal advanced during the campaign was conformity to principles, i.e., conformity to the past, since the principles are supposed to have proved themselves, one way or the other, during the past. Such appeals are probably good both ways; that is, they are good *for* the propagandist because of their convenient adaptability (almost anything can be shown to conform to or oppose some "historical principle") and they are good *on* the voters because of the strong emotional appeal exercised by the familiar past and its symbols. Psychologists could discourse on this appeal's subjective role (its roots in infancy, etc.) and sociologists could discourse on its social role (its conserving influence, etc.). At any rate, it constituted the dominant social value in terms of which the candidates attempted to sell their programs.

The Means: The Less Said . . .

In addition to talking about the goals and results of their policies, the candidates and their spokesmen had to say something about the methods by which their policies, or their opponents' policies, would be realized. Actually, not much was said. Only 14% of the total material contained references to methods, and that was often either irrelevant or vague. In other words, there was little inclination on either side to intrude much discussion of *how* their programs would be realized upon the more desirable (and less controversial) discussion of the attractive programs themselves.

Emotional Terms: The Labels of the Campaign

All sorts of propaganda rely on emotional appeals to get their message across. Such appeals are usually embodied in the use of various sentimentalized terms—symbols which the people are strongly for or against, like democracy and communism. In 1940, such terms were found in virtually every sentence of campaign propaganda. There was twice as much use of them in late October as in early August; they kept pace with the rising intensity of the campaign. Furthermore, material dealing with Roosevelt—whether pro or con—contained more emotional heat than parallel topics dealing with Willkie. Evidently the president was more "loved" and "hated" than his opponent.

CHAPTER XIV

The Radio and the Printed Page

A presidential election means a presidential campaign, and that means a flood-tide of political propaganda. Campaign managers devise comprehensive strategies and ingenious tactics in an attempt to make their will the will of the electorate. Party workers adapt general policy to specific situations in an effort to corral the timid, lead the willing, and convince the reluctant. Partisan leaders of opinion—the newspaper editor, the columnist, the free lance writer and the syndicated cartoonist, the radio commentator, and the local sage—all edge into the campaign by placing the weight of their authority behind the cause of their favored candidate. Propaganda is let loose upon the land to control or inform, to constrain or tease potential voters into the appropriate decision.

Thus the *output* of campaign propaganda is tremendous. But what of the *intake?* Unheard music may be sweeter, but unseen or unheard propaganda is simply useless. How much actual attention is paid to it? By whom? In which media of communication? In short, what about actual exposure to campaign propaganda?

Most people have several claims upon their attention and interest which necessarily compete with one another. There is competition between the problems of their "private world" and those of the "public world." Pre-occupation with personal problems does not leave much time or energy for concern with such relatively remote issues as the choice of a president. And even within the world of public affairs, no single focus of attention remains unchallenged. For example, the campaign of

1940 had to compete for attention with a series of major events which have not marked a presidential campaign since 1916—a European war.

As everyone knows, the intensity of a presidential campaign hits its high point just before Election Day when all the media of mass communication—newspapers, magazines and radio—are filled with political propaganda. If people are ever going to read about the campaign or listen to political speeches, this is the time.[1] How many actually did? In Erie County, during the last twelve days of the campaign, 54% of the respondents had heard at least one of five major political talks broadcast in the days just before the interview, 51% had read at least one campaign story which had appeared on the front page of their favorite newspaper the day before the interview, and 26% had read at least one campaign article in the current mass magazines. This is important. At the peak of the campaign, in late October, about half the population ignored stories on the front page of their newspapers or political speeches by the candidates themselves, and about 75% of the people ignored magazine stories about the election. In short, the flood of political material at that time, far from drowning any of these people, did not even get their feet wet.

The Concentration of Exposure

But this interpretation might miss the mark. Although half the respondents were not exposed to any *one* source, perhaps all of them, or nearly all, were exposed to *some* source. In other words, perhaps the people *specialized* in their exposure to communication, some reading but not listening and others listening but not reading. And thus perhaps everyone was exposed to the campaign somewhere.

Actually, however, the opposite is the case. With remarkable consistency, political materials distributed through the various media of communication reached the *same* group of potential voters.[2] The people who were exposed to a lot of campaign propaganda through one medium of communication

were also exposed to a lot in the other media; and those who
were exposed to a little in one were also exposed to a little in
the others. Most of the people above average in their exposure
to political speeches over the radio were also above average in
their exposure to political material in newspapers (Chart 33).
The same relationship holds for newspapers and magazines and
for radio and magazines. And conversely, the people who were
low in exposure to one medium were also low in the others.

CHART 33

*People highly exposed to one medium of communication
also tend to be highly exposed to other media. There are
relatively few who are highly exposed to one medium
and little exposed to the other.*

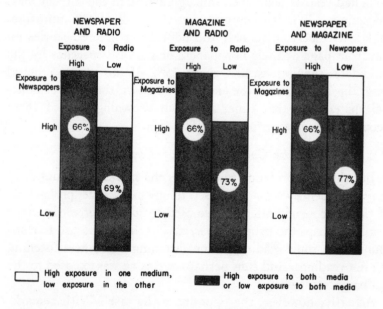

Exposure to the different media of political communications,
then, is concentrated in the same group. But what of exposure at different times during the campaign? Perhaps some
people read and listened during the first months of the cam-

paign and others during the last months—and thus perhaps everyone was exposed to about the same amount of political propaganda over the campaign as a whole. Again, however, this is just not so. Again the same group of people were highly exposed at different periods of the campaign and another group of people were little exposed at different periods in the campaign (Chart 34).[3]

CHART 34

People highly exposed at one time also tend to be highly exposed at another time of the campaign.

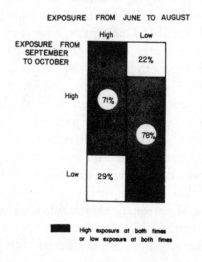

EXPOSURE FROM JUNE TO AUGUST

High   Low

EXPOSURE FROM
SEPTEMBER
TO OCTOBER

22%

High   71%

78%

Low   29%

High exposure at both times
or low exposure at both times

In sum, then, exposure to political communications during the presidential campaign is concentrated in the *same* group of people, not spread among the people at large. Exposure in one medium or at one time *supplements* rather than complements exposure in another medium or at another time. The large and increasing supply of political propaganda during the campaign leads primarily not to a wider base of informed voters but to a more intensive dosage of the same part of the electorate.

Who Read and Listened to Politics

Who were the people who did most of the reading about and listening to the campaign? What distinguished them from the people who paid little attention to politics?

The primary distinction between people who saw and heard a lot of campaign propaganda and those who saw and heard only a little was their interest in the election. This has been mentioned in Chapter V, and need only be noted for the record here.

The interested were highly exposed, and so were the decided. At any one time, the people who already knew how they were going to vote read and listened to more campaign material than the people who still did not know how they would vote. In other words, the group which the campaign manager is presumably most eager to reach—the as-yet undecided—is the very group which is less likely to read or listen to his propaganda. Just as educational programs on the air attract an audience largely composed of those previously familiar with their contents, so does political propaganda tend to reach an audience that has already decided on its choice of a candidate.

In the chapter dealing with the role of interest in the election, we saw that interest serves as a synoptic index for an entire complex of personal characteristics. The most interested people were better-educated, better-off, older, urban men. These same characteristics are associated with high exposure to political communications. There are good cultural reasons to explain this. The better-educated have more intellectual equipment and more civic training. The better-off have a greater awareness about politics and think they have a larger stake in it. The older also think they have a bigger stake in politics; in addition, the younger people in this country, unlike the youth of Europe, are not particularly politically conscious. The urban find it easier to expose to communications, especially print, because there are more opportunities to do so in the city than in the country. And finally, men are compelled by the mores to pay attention to politics and women are not.

Obviously, the people who expose most to campaign communications are those who possessed all three factors: interest, decision, and the appropriate personal characteristics.[4] But what about their relative importance? Cross-analysis reveals that exposure to campaign communications was determined primarily by interest in the election; secondly by a vote decision; and finally by education, economic status, and sex and to a lesser extent by age and residence.

In summary, then, the relative strength of these factors highlights an important fact about exposure to political communications. We will recall that the people with most interest were most likely to make their vote decision early and stick to it throughout the campaign. What we find now is that the people who did most of the reading about and listening to the campaign were the most impervious to any ideas which might have led them to change their vote. Insofar as campaign propaganda was intended to change votes, it was most likely to reach the people least susceptible to such changes. It was least likely to reach the people most likely to change.

Which Is More Influential—Radio or Newspaper?

In recent years, the radio has taken its place beside the newspaper as a distinctive medium of communication. Perhaps not just "beside"; perhaps in some instances the radio has taken the place *of* the newspaper. For example, has the radio cut into the newspaper's sphere of influence in American politics? Did the two media serve the same function for the major parties? In short, what were their comparative political roles in Erie County in 1940?[5]

Before attacking this question directly, we must digress for a brief methodological note. Suppose we asked the respondents themselves to indicate what sources were most effective in influencing their vote decision. Merely raising the question is enough to call to mind the dangers involved in such a procedure. Can respondents appraise the relative influences exerted upon them over an extended period of time? Any statement by them to the effect that they were "influenced" by the "radio" or "newspaper" may refer as much to the *amount* of listening or reading they have done as to the *actual influence* of the media. A direct self-estimate by respondents, then, will not serve our purpose.

Accordingly, a method of investigation was devised which rests on the following assumption: the more concrete and specific the respondent's account of the experiences which have modified his view, the more likely it is that the account is valid. General comments may inadvertently refer to amount of exposure and not to influence. But concrete and circumstantial reports of specific experiences tend to focus on decisive events and to eliminate the component of amount of exposure. Obviously, no single question can be expected to provide an adequate index of influence. But we can use a battery of questions which enable us to distinguish between general and vague replies on the one hand and concrete replies on the other. If we find that the influence attributed to one medium is consistently mentioned more frequently as we move from general to specific replies, then we conclude that this medium has actually exerted a preponderant influence and that we have arrived at a valid measure of influence.

With that procedure and that measure, what was the comparative influence of radio and newspaper in the 1940 campaign? Just after the election, voters were asked to name in retrospect the sources from which they obtained most of the information that led them to arrive at their vote decision. They were then asked to indicate which source proved most important to them. Although the radio and newspaper ranked about the same as general sources, the radio was mentioned half again as frequently as the single most important source of influence (Chart 35). Half of those who mentioned the radio at all considered it their most important source of information, whereas only a third of those who initially mentioned the newspaper regarded it as most important. Thus, as we move from the more general to the more specific indication of influence, radio plays a relatively stronger role than the newspaper. The same sort of distinction can be applied to another set of data.

CHART 35

Asked which medium helped them to make their decision, the voters mention radio and newspaper about equally. When they are asked for the "most important" source, however, radio gets a clear lead.

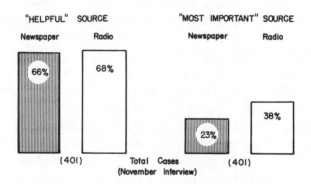

"HELPFUL" SOURCE   "MOST IMPORTANT" SOURCE

Newspaper   Radio   Newspaper   Radio

66%   68%   23%   38%

(401)   Total Cases   (401)
(November Interview)

Radio and Newspaper as Sources of Reasons for Change

Whenever a respondent indicated a vote intention different from the one mentioned in the previous interview, he was asked the reason for the change. In some cases the source of the new vote intention was stated in *general* terms, e.g., "I changed my mind as a result of my newspaper reading." In other cases, the source of the change was reported in *concrete* terms, with a medium of communications *directly linked* to the reason for change, e.g., "An editorial in Wednesday's Sandusky *News* convinced me that the president's experience in international affairs was indispensable." (We should note here that whereas in the preceding section we dealt with the respondents as a whole, here we deal only with the crucial sub-group—the people who changed their minds during the campaign.) When the mentions of media making for changes in vote intention are classified as general and concrete, how did newspaper and radio compare?

Until the last period of the campaign, considerably more political material was available in the newspapers than on the radio. Although it is difficult to measure this factor of accessibility, only toward the close of the campaign could the amount of political material on the air be considered at all comparable to that found in the press. If we limit mentions of media in connection with reasons for change to the last two months of the campaign—the most active months of the campaign—what then?

At that time the radio was mentioned less frequently as a *general* source of influence but more frequently as a *concrete* source. Once again, the stronger role of radio becomes more conspicuous in the case of concrete ascriptions of influence.

In sum, to the extent that the formal media exerted any influence at all on vote intention or actual vote, radio proved more effective than the newspaper. Differences in the way the campaign is waged in print and on the air probably account for this. In the first place, a considerable amount of political matrial appears in the press from the beginning to the end of the campaign with few notable variations. In time, the claims and counter-claims of the parties as they appeared in cold print came to pall upon the reader who had been exposed to essentially the same stuff over an extended period. The campaign on the radio, however, was much more cursory in its early phases and became vigorous and sustained only toward the close.

Secondly, the radio campaign consists much more of "events" of distinctive interest. A political convention is broadcast, and the listener can virtually participate in the ceremonial occasion: he can respond to audience enthusiasm, he can directly experience the ebb and flow of tension. Similarly with a major speech by one of the candidates: it is more dramatic than the same speech in the newspaper next morning.

And thirdly, the listener gets a sense of personal access from the radio which is absent from print. Politics on the air more readily becomes an active experience for the listener than politics in the newspaper does for the reader. It represents an approach to a face-to-face contact with the principals in the case. It is closer to a personal relationship, and hence more effective.

A Medium For Each Party

In 1936 and even more in 1940, most of the country's newspapers supported the Republican candidate for the presidency (and the same was true in Sandusky.) And in both campaigns, according to popular legend, Roosevelt's "superb radio voice" enabled him to exploit that medium far more effectively than either Landon or Willkie. Thus, broadly speaking, it would appear that each party had an effective hold on one of the two major media of communication.

This was actually the case. In exposure, in congeniality of ideas, in trust, and in influence—in all of these characteristics the Republicans inclined in favor of the newspaper and the Democrats in favor of the radio. Among people with the same amounts of formal education, the Republicans read the newspaper more than the Democrats and the Democrats listened to the radio more than the Republicans (Chart 36). When we recall the finding in Chapter XIII that the pro-Republican content of the newspapers was higher than that on the air, this suggests once more that people tend to seek out political views similar to their own. And our respondents were aware of the facts in the case: when asked, in late October, where they found "ideas on the coming election which agree most closely with your own ideas," the Republicans favored the newspaper and the Democrats favored the radio, relatively speaking (Chart 37).

What about the implications? Again in late October, re-

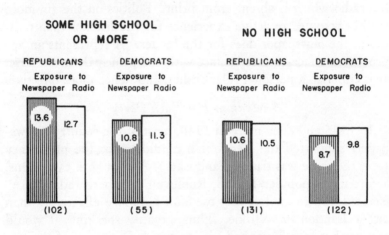

CHART 36

Republican voters expose themselves more to newspapers and Democratic voters more to radio, on each educational level.

SOME HIGH SCHOOL OR MORE

NO HIGH SCHOOL

REPUBLICANS — Exposure to Newspaper Radio
DEMOCRATS — Exposure to Newspaper Radio
REPUBLICANS — Exposure to Newspaper Radio
DEMOCRATS — Exposure to Newspaper Radio

13.6 12.7   (102)
10.8 11.3   (55)
10.6 10.5   (131)
8.7 9.8   (122)

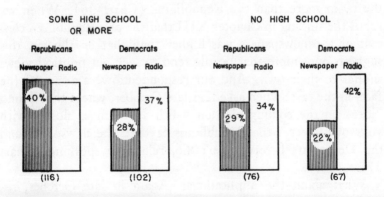

CHART 37

Republicans find the newspaper relatively more consistent with their own ideas and the Democrats the radio, on each educational level.

SOME HIGH SCHOOL OR MORE

NO HIGH SCHOOL

Republicans — Newspaper Radio
Democrats — Newspaper Radio
Republicans — Newspaper Radio
Democrats — Newspaper Radio

40%   (116)
28% 37%   (102)
29% 34%   (76)
22% 42%   (67)

spondents were asked which they thought was "closer to the truth (more impartial)—the news you get in the newspapers or what you hear on the radio?" Again, relatively, the partisans ascribed "impartiality" and "veracity" to the media which presented views similar to their own (Chart 38). A transfer was effected from partisan value to truth value.

This tendency was virtually confined to the better-educated respondents. They were more sensitized to the partisanship of the media and responded with distrust of the veracity of the "rival" source of information. The less educated were less likely to detect the partisan character of the media and hence less likely to discount them accordingly.

And finally, the influence of the two media was different for the two parties (Chart 39). People changing their vote intentions favorably for the Republicans mentioned newspapers more frequently as the source of their reason for change and Democrats mentioned the radio more frequently (taking the more reliable concrete mentions only).

In summary, then, Republicans preferred the newspaper and Democrats the radio. Each party exposed more to "its own" medium, found it more congenial, trusted it more, and was more influenced by it.

In spite of the fact that the content of the radio favored the Republicans, the radio more often impressed people in favor of the Democratic party. Some of the reasons for this are clear. When radio commentators and newscasters were cited by our respondents, it was not so much because of their broadcasts on domestic politics but because of their reports on foreign affairs and war news. Under the circumstances, these worked to the advantage of the Democrats. Take, for example, the young woman who returned to a Democratic vote because of a newscast: "FDR knows the European situation as well as any man. *I heard a news report that Hitler and Mussolini want FDR defeated.* If they do, it's for their own benefit, so I will vote for FDR if only to spite the dictators."

CHART 38

Republicans also thought the newspaper was relatively more impartial (closer to the truth) than the radio and the Democrats favored the radio, again on each educational level.

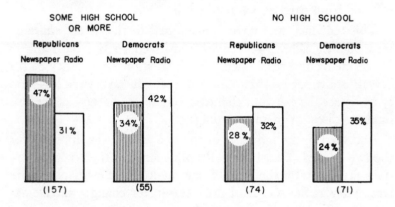

SOME HIGH SCHOOL OR MORE

Republicans — Newspaper Radio — 47% / 31% — (157)

Democrats — Newspaper Radio — 34% / 42% — (55)

NO HIGH SCHOOL

Republicans — Newspaper Radio — 28% / 32% — (74)

Democrats — Newspaper Radio — 24% / 35% — (71)

CHART 39

People changing towards the Republicans mention newspapers more often as an influence which led to the change and those changing towards the Democrats mention radio.

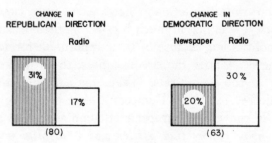

CHANGE IN REPUBLICAN DIRECTION — Radio — 31% / 17% — (80)

CHANGE IN DEMOCRATIC DIRECTION — Newspaper Radio — 20% / 30% — (63)

Height of bar indicates number of times newspaper ▥ or radio ▭ is mentioned as main source of change.

The radio speeches of the candidates themselves also helped the Democrats. All three of the respondents who mentioned a Roosevelt speech in connection with a change in vote intention shifted toward the Democrats. Similarly, all four of the respondents who mentioned both Roosevelt and Willkie speeches were persuaded to vote Democratic. But of the eight respondents who mentioned speeches by Willkie, four decided to vote for Roosevelt. In other words, Willkie's speeches were as likely to boomerang against him as they were to operate in his favor. For example, this young man, after vacillating between the parties, finally decided for Roosevelt in October: *"I have heard some of Willkie's speeches and I don't like him. . . .* All he does is condemn Roosevelt. He doesn't say how he will do things if he gets elected. Roosevelt has never said anything against Willkie."

On the other hand, the speeches by the President did not affect any changers adversely. The typical reaction is illustrated in the case of this elderly woman who was undecided right up to the last days of the campaign: *"Since I heard President Roosevelt's speech from Philadelphia* I have decided that Willkie has not had enough experience to be president. He doesn't know enough about the war situation." And Roosevelt had much the better of it whenever the respondents listened to both men and compared them. For example, here is a young man who finally decided to vote Democratic: *"Willkie's and Roosevelt's speeches on Saturday night made me decide to vote for FDR.* They were the first speeches I heard. Willkie is no speaker—he knocks too much."

Thus Roosevelt's "good" radio manner and Willkie's "bad" radio manner, often discussed during the campaign, actually paid off. One should remember that most of these changers were only activated and not converted by what they heard on the radio. Still, such experiences clarify why the radio was considered more the Democrats' medium as compared with the newspaper.

The Magazine—Specialized Medium of Communication

Turning finally to the weekly and monthly journals, we find another picture. A presidential campaign provides American magazines with a central event around which articles can be planned and written for a period of months, and they take good advantage of it. Throughout the campaign, the mass magazines carried a good deal of political discussion of election issues and particularly of the candidates' personalities, as we have seen in the preceding chapter.

The possibility of magazine influence upon vote is limited at the outset by the relatively small numbers of magazine readers. As indicated in Footnote 1 to this chapter, only 15% to 25% of the respondents read magazine articles on the campaign at any one time.

But the small size of the magazine audience is somewhat off-set by its characteristics. As indicated in Chapter V, we found a small proportion of politically active and alert people in each social group who were likely to influence the decision of their fellow citizens—the opinion leaders. Among other differences, they read more about the campaign and also listened more. Such differences between the opinion leaders and the rest of the people are especially marked in regard to magazine reading. On our index of exposure we find that the average opinion leader has about twice as high a score as the ordinary citizen with reference to newspapers and radio. But with magazine reading, the difference is almost three to one.

The highpoint of the magazine's influence came relatively early in the campaign in question. At that time, the newspapers and radio are relatively free of campaign material because not much is going on, and the magazines fill the breach with "time-less" articles such as reviews of the challenger's career. Most of the mentions of magazines as sources connected with reasons for change came during the first half of the campaign. And the magazine is probably relatively more important during the pre-convention period of late spring, before our interviewing began.

But once the campaign reaches its height, in middle and late October, the magazine takes even more of a back seat to newspaper and radio.

Two tendencies in particular characterize the political role of magazines: (1) they deal largely with personalities[6] and (2) they have more space to devote to the elaboration of a point. The preceding chapter showed the extent to which magazines stressed the personalities of the candidates, particularly Willkie's. This emphasis on personality also came out in the citation of magazines in connection with the reasons for change in vote intention. More often than not, it was the character of the Republican candidate or his career or some other aspect of the man himself, rather than his program, which was cited. Such testimony appeared often: "Read a sketch of Willkie's life in the *Saturday Evening Post*. . . . Read about Willkie's life in the *Farm Journal*. . . ."

At the same time, there were suggestions in the citation of sources that the magazine was relatively more likely to supply elaborations of a point than either the newspaper or the radio. It is less tied to current events than the newspaper and it can take more time to develop a point than the usual political speaker, who tries to cover a good many topics within one talk. No definitive evidence is available on this matter, but hints of it appeared from time to time in the interviews. For example, here is a woman who decided to vote Republican in June because she thought Dewey would get the nomination: "I like Dewey, from what I have read—his *cleaning up the gangsters*, etc. I read an article in the *American* about *the life and background* of Dewey, and *his work on crime* in New York City."

As a source of influence, the specialized magazine designed for a special-interest audience rivalled the general mass magazine. The latter have many times the coverage of the former but they are relatively less effective in changing peoples' minds. The specialized magazine already has a foot in the door, so to speak, because it is accepted by the reader as a reliable spokesman for some cause or group in which he is greatly interested and with which he identifies himself. The general magazine tries to speak to everyone at once and as a result is less able to aim its shots directly at a particular target. In addition, the general magazine is ordinarily considered as an entertainment publication whereas specialized magazines are granted a serious turn. In Erie County in 1940, the *Farm Journal* was mentioned as a concrete influence upon changes in vote intention as frequently as *Collier's*, despite their great difference in circulation, and the Townsend publication as frequently as *Life* or the *Saturday Evening Post*.

This chapter provides a general idea of the role played by the formal media of communications in the 1940 campaign. Now we turn to the face-to-face contacts among the people themselves.

CHAPTER XV

The Political Homogeneity of Social Groups

Repeatedly in this study we found indications that people vote "in groups." In this chapter we shall focus upon the importance of this aspect of voting.

As the reader will remember, slightly more than half of Erie County voters were Republican. This was true for the total population of the county, as well as for the different groups of 600 people included in our study. If, then, we had taken the name of every hundredth person from an alphabetical list of all county residents, we would have found, again, that slightly more than half were Republicans.

But suppose now we had proceeded differently, had picked a score of Republicans at random, and had asked them to name as many friends, neighbors, and fellow workers as they could remember. If we then asked the people assembled on this list for whom they intended to vote, the proportion of Republicans would have been considerably higher than it was for the county as a whole. And, conversely, if we had started with a score of Democrats and had asked them to name their associates in the different spheres of their lives, we would have found a considerably lower proportion of Republicans on this list than we found in the county.

This represents another formulation of our statement that voting is essentially a group experience. People who work or live or play together are likely to vote for the same candidates.

Two kinds of evidence may be provided for this general statement. On the one hand we can study directly the political homogeneity of such groups as fraternal organizations, churches, sports clubs as well as the family and similar institutionalized groups. On the other hand we can use an indirect approach. People who have certain characteristics in common are more likely to belong to the same groups. We know from general observation, for instance, that people tend to associate with others of their own age rather than with people considerably older or younger than themselves. If we find then that there are marked differences in voting between various age groups, we would have inferential evidence that people who have closer contacts with each other are more apt to vote alike.[1]

Social Stratification and Political Homogeneity

Beginning with this second and inferential approach, we find our best lead in those factors on which our index of political predisposition was based (Chapter III)—SES level, religious affiliation, and residence.

Each of these three factors plays an important role in deciding what type of people will have close personal contact with each other. Farmers are more likely to see farmers whereas they have less contact with urban people who, in turn, live more among themselves. The same is true for groups of people on different socio-economic levels. Common experiences, as well as precise studies, show that an individual chooses his friends and finds his neighbors on about his own SES level. As a matter of fact, our urban social institutions such as clubs, neighborhoods, restaurants, and informal social gatherings bring together people of similar socio-economic status and contribute to socially stratified living. Finally, common religious affiliation not only brings people together at church affairs, but is likely to influence marital choice and may affect employment.

Thus, what we have said before can be reformulated in the following fashion: People who have similar ratings according to the index of political predispositions (IPP) are also likely to live in closer contact with each other. And, the groups which they form are likely to be rather homogeneous in political outlook and behavior.

This tendency is accentuated during the course of the campaign. If we use our IPP ratings as an index of the groups to which people belong, then the changes in vote intention increase group homogeneity. Table IX has classified the 54 changers according to their IPP ratings. If, first, we look at their May vote intentions, we find that 60% of them (the 24 cases with "Republican" IPP ratings who intended to vote Democratic, and the 10 "Democrats" who intended to vote Republican) were deviates. In the October interview, these same individuals had adjusted their vote intention so that it was consistent with their IPP ratings. The remaining 40% had become deviates. In other words, the proportion of deviates among the changers had been reduced by 20% between May and October. Thus, the majority of voters who change at all change in the direction of the prevailing vote of their social groups.[2]

TABLE IX: THE PARTY CHANGERS AND THEIR
POLITICAL PREDISPOSITIONS

	Kind of Change in Vote Intention	
IPP	Democratic-Republican	Republican-Democratic
"Republican" _____	24	4
"Democratic" _____	16	10

This result remains substantially the same if we add two control groups, for which we can study the changes between May and July and between May and August.[3]

To the extent that the campaign brings about changes in vote intention, then, these changes operate to increase the political homogeneity of social groups. Upon further scrutiny, it turns out that the people themselves are quite aware that the campaign reshuffles their environment so that, politically, it becomes more consistent with their own views. At the last interview before the election, we asked the following question: "Looking back at the campaign so far, how many people among your friends and relatives have changed their minds on how they will probably vote? In which direction did they change?"

In order to have a clearer picture of the situation, we studied the responses of only those people who had a constant vote intention and who did not vote in the November elections. What did these people observe going on around them? The answer is given in Table X.

TABLE X: DIRECTION OF CHANGES NOTICED BY DIFFERENT
GROUPS OF RESPONDENTS

	Majority Changed to FDR	WW	None[4]	Total
Republicans	2%	54%	44%	100%
Democrats	17	22	61	100
"Don't Knows"	7	21	72	100

As we see from this table, each of the two major political environments operates as a kind of magnetic force, drawing to it people of like outlook, and rejecting individuals of dissimilar viewpoint. In other words, each group becomes slowly but surely more homogeneous in political opinion and behavior. The changes taking place around Republican observers are, in a majority of the cases, in a Republican direction. And, conversely, wherever changes in favor of Roosevelt are noticed, they are reported by Democratic observers.

It might be argued that this result can be entirely explained by the mechanism of projection—that our observers saw only those changes which favored the candidates of their choice. Table X shows that this is not the case, however. For the Democratic as well as the Republican respondents observed more changes in favor of Willkie. And this indicates the realistic nature of our respondents' observations, for it is known that the county became more and more Republican as the campaign progressed.

The Political Structure of the Family

The family is a group particularly suited to the purposes of our study, because here living conditions attain a maximum of similarity and because mutual contacts are more frequent than in other groupings.

In August we found 344 panel members who had made up their minds as to how they would vote, and who also had another eligible voter living in the same household. At that time,

78% of these other eligible voters intended to vote for the same candidate as did the respondent, 20% were uncertain, and 2% disagreed with the respondent in his choice of candidate. The situation changed little when it came to actual voting. After the election, only 4% of the 413 panel members who 'voted claimed that someone in their families had voted differently from themselves.[5] It is interesting to observe, incidentally, that the extent of disagreement increased slightly toward the end of the campaign. This is consistent with the results of Chapter VI where we saw that people under cross-pressure make their final vote intention late.

We can explore the inter-relationships of influence within the family in somewhat greater detail. Among husbands and wives, both of whom had decided to vote, only one pair in 22 disagreed. Among parents and children, one pair in 12 disagreed, the gap of a generation increasing differences in life and outlook. Agreement was least—as all the jokes emphasize —among "in-laws" living in the same household. One pair in five showed disagreement on party alignment.

The almost perfect agreement between husband and wife comes about as a result of male dominance in political situations. At one point of the study we asked each respondent whether he had discussed politics with someone else in recent weeks. Forty-five of the women stated that they had talked the election over with their husbands; but, of an equal number of randomly selected men, only four reported discussions with their wives. If these family discussions play as important a role for husbands as they do for wives, then we should get approximately the same number of reports on the interchange of political ideas from both sexes. But only the wives are aware of the political opinions of their husbands. Men do not feel that they are discussing politics with their wives; they feel they are telling them. And, as we can see from the following quotations, the wives are willing to be told:

"On previous interviews, I hadn't given it any thought, but it is close to election and I guess I will vote Democratic and *go along with my husband."*

"My husband has always been Republican. He says that if we vote for different parties there is no use in our voting. So *I think I will give in this year and vote Republican. . . ."*

It appears that not only the color of opinion, but the whole level of interest is contagious from one family member to another. Of the men who had a vote intention and great interest in the election, only 30% claimed that their wives did not intend to vote, or did not know for whom. For men with less interest, the figure is 52%.

If the relationships between father and daughter or between brother and sister are studied, we find a similar dominance of the male in political matters.

In addition, the political homogeneity of the family may extend over several generations. Our panel members were asked, "Do you consider that your family (parents, grandparents) have always been predominantly Democratic or predominantly Republican?" Fully three-fourths of the respondents with vote intentions in September followed the political lead of their families. Here are examples of two *first voters* who took over the family pattern at the very beginning of their voting careers:

"Probably will vote Democratic because *my grandfather will skin me if I don't."*

"If I can register I will vote Republican because *my family are all Republicans so therefore I would have to vote that way."*

These young voters, one a man and the other a woman, provide excellent illustrations of family influence. Neither had much interest in the election and neither paid much attention to the campaign. Both accepted family tradition for their first votes and both are likely to remain in line with that tradition. In the first case, there is even a hint that family sanctions are used to enforce the decision. Thus are party voters born.

Now, what of the exceptional cases in which disagreement does occur within the family? A number of respondents agreed with the young voter just quoted, that political conformity is the price of domestic peace. There was evidence of a good deal of tension in families which could not reach an agreement.

One girl reported in June she intended to vote for the Democratic party because she "liked the Democratic candidates better than the Republicans." She "read an article in *Collier's* about the Republican candidates and didn't think they sounded very interesting." She "felt Roosevelt did a good job as president" and approved the third term. The girl's parents, however, favored the Republican candidate and this was the source of much conflict. The girl's mother told the interviewer: "She just does it to be opposite. I have always felt that *her views were just revolt against tradition and the stuffy ideas of her parents.*"

The respondent finally broke down and voted for Willkie, explaining, "*My father and friends* thought it would be a good idea not to have Roosevelt for a third term because he would be too much of a dictator."

It is reasonable to expect that with such pressure toward homogeneity, people with unhomogeneous family backgrounds will be more uncertain about their own political affiliations. Chart 40 compares the amount of shifting of political position by respondents from families with different degrees of homogeneity in vote intention.

Less than 3% of voters in families homogeneous in August changed their vote intention during the rest of the campaign. But if there were some relatives who were undecided (the second group in Chart 40) almost 10% of the respondents shifted between August and October. And in the small group of families in which there was definite disagreement, 29% of the respondents went through at least one change in position.

And when the people in families not homogeneous in their vote intentions did change their minds, they changed toward the party favored by the rest of the family. Fully 81% of the members of Republican families who were originally undecided were pro-Republican in October; and 71% of those in Democratic families later came out for Roosevelt. Whatever the reason, whether honest conviction or family loyalty, the family molded their votes—and as a result the family became politically more homogeneous as the campaign wore on.

CHART 40

The less homogeneous the family is with respect to their votes, the more the members of the family tend to change their minds.

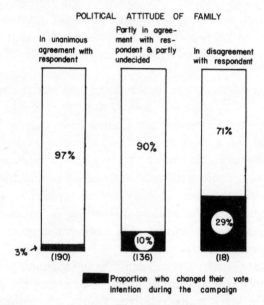

POLITICAL   ATTITUDE   OF   FAMILY

In unanimous agreement with respondent

Partly in agreement with respondent & partly undecided

In disagreement with respondent

71%

90%

97%

29%

10%

3% →   (190)   (136)   (18)

■ Proportion who changed their vote intention during the campaign

Again, if all the family members were undecided about their vote intention in August, 63% of the respondents from these families were still undecided two months later. But if anyone in the family had reached a decision in August, the proportion of respondents remaining undecided two months later was only 48%. In other words, the person who lives in a family where members have decided their vote intention is much more likely to make up his own mind before Election Day than is the person who lives in a family where no one has a clearcut vote intention.

The family, then, provided a very definite climate of political influence. All of its members are inclined to vote in the same way, and in those cases where there is disagreement, the tension of the situation leads the family members to make some adjustments. It is usually the women who so adjust, and it is from them that we get most of the references to family discussions as sources of change.

There is no reason why other social groups should not be studied in the same way. The higher level of political tension created during the campaign gives us an opportunity to find out how this political homogeneity of social groups comes about. It is to some of the finer aspects of this process that we now turn.

The Role of Formal Associations

Our sample was too small to make feasible a study of specific organizations. But we can distinguish between those people who belong to formal organizations and those who do not. There are two general findings with regard to membership in these formal organizations which are as applicable to Erie County as they are to other American communities which have been studied before. In the first place, we find that the members of any given organization are recruited from fairly similar socioeconomic levels. Secondly, people on the lower SES levels are less likely to belong to any organizations than the people on high SES levels. (On the A and B level, we find that 72% of these respondents belong to one or more organizations. The proportion of respondents who are members of formal organizations decreases steadily as SES level descends until, on the D level, only 35% of the respondents belong to any associations.)[6]

With these two results in mind, what differences between members and non-members of such organizations does our main thesis lead us to expect? We anticipate that on each SES level the social predisposition of organization members will be more strongly activated than is that of those people on the same SES levels who are not subject to the "molecular pressures" of the associations. This, we must realize, will be possible only so long as the comparison is carried out on each separate SES level.

Although the proportion of Republicans is generally great on high SES levels, the Republican trend is still stronger among those who join various associations (Chart 41). Why? Is it not likely that simply meeting more often with other persons, even in organizations not ostensibly concerned with politics, brings about a greater activation of predispositions?

CHART 41

On the three higher SES levels, membership in a social or similar organization reinforces the tendency to vote Republican. On the lowest SES level, membership makes almost no difference.

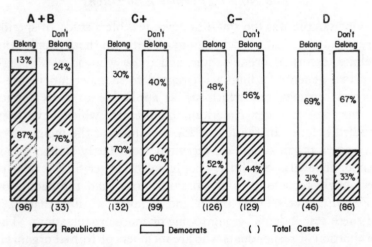

But at the low end of the socio-economic scale, our thesis does not seem to hold true at first glance. According to our thesis, those people on low SES levels who become members of associations should, by association with others of like status, be activated toward a Democratic vote intention. That trend is not quite so apparent in Chart 41, however. It is true that on the D level those active in organizations are a little less likely to be Republicans and somewhat more likely to be Democrats. But the difference is slight. And on the C— level, the effect of participation is still in the direction of Republicanism.

Our thesis is not refuted by these results, however. For reference to the second characteristic of these organizations explains the irregularities in Chart 41 and clarifies the whole situation. Any people of C— or D level who belong to these organizations constitute only a small minority, and are naturally influenced by the higher prestige of the dominant group.

The truth of our expectation about the normal tendency of organizations—that they activate the latent predispositions of members—can be seen clearly, however, if we study a type of organization which is limited to people of the C— or D level. As we stated above, there are few such groups in Sandusky, but the trade unions do meet our criterion. In his union the worker of C— or D economic level associates with, and is stimulated by, others of like predisposition. As a result, we find that on the C— and D levels, only 31% of those who were union members but 53% of those who were not union members voted Republican.

Politically, then, formal associations have a class character. They facilitate the transformation of social characteristics into political affiliations. But, conversely, our results show that the prestige values within the organizations may, in the case of minority members, operate to develop political affiliations which are opposed to the predispositions of these members.

Bringing Opinions Into Line

One final observation demonstrates that during the campaign social groups imbue their individual members with the accepted political ideology of the group. By and large, people who intend to vote for a certain party agree with its main tenets. Republicans, as we have seen, do not approve of the third term, have a high opinion of Willkie, think that business experience is more important than government experience, etc. Democrats feel the other way around on all these issues. But in the middle of the campaign, in August, there were still a number of people who had an inconsistent attitude pattern. There were, for instance, 33 Republicans who felt that government experience is more important in a president, and 30 Democrats who thought that business experience would be more desirable. (For further data on this, see Chapter IV). In the course of the campaign there was a tendency toward consistency. More than half (33) of the people just mentioned achieved harmony between vote intention and opinion on this specific question by October. But how did this come about? Did people finally join the party which conformed to their ideas or did they take over the prevailing opinion of the political group to which they belonged? This answer is very clear-cut. Thirty retained their party allegiance but changed their vote intention to fit their theory.[7]

This is consistently true for whatever specific opinion we take. Inconsistencies are reduced, but in such a way that people stick to their vote intention and start to think about specific issues in the way the majority of their fellow partisans do. These results fit very well into what we have said before. If a person's vote intention is to a great degree a symbol of the social group to which he or she belongs, then we should not be surprised that people iron out inconsistencies in their thinking in such a way as to conform to the group with which they live from day to day. In a way, the content of this chapter can be summarized by saying that people vote, not only *with* their social group, but also *for* it.

Vote Decision as a Social Experience

How may we explain the fact that social groups are politically homogeneous and that the campaign increases this homogeneity still more? There is, first, the fact that people who live together under similar external conditions are likely to develop similar needs and interests. They tend to see the world through the same colored glasses; they tend to apply to common experiences common interpretations. They will approve of a political candidate who has achieved success in their own walk of life; they will approve of programs which are couched in terms taken from their own occupations and adapted to the moral standards of the groups in which they have a common "belonging."

But this is only part of the picture. There may be many group members who are not really aware of the goals of their own group. And there may be many who, even if they were aware of these goals, would not be sufficiently interested in current events to tie the two together consciously. They acquiesce to the political temper of their group under the steady, personal influence of their more politically active fellow citizens. Here again, we find the process of activation by which the predisposed attitudes of some are brought out by the influence of others. But, in addition, we see here the direct effectiveness of personal contacts. It is these which we must study in specific detail.

CHAPTER XVI

The Nature of Personal Influence

The political homogeneity of social groups is promoted by personal relationships among the same kinds of people. But for a detailed and systematic study of the influence of such relationships—the political role of personal influence—a systematic inventory would be needed of the various personal contacts and political discussions that people had over a sample number of days. That would provide an index of personal exposure similar to the indices of exposure to the formal media developed in previous chapters. Such complete data are not available in the present study,[1] but enough information has been collected to indicate the importance of personal relationships so far as their direct political influence is concerned. Our findings and impressions will be summarized without much formal statistical data. The significance of this area of political behavior was highlighted by the study but further investigation is necessary to establish it more firmly.

In comparison with the formal media of communication, personal relationships are potentially more influential for two reasons: their coverage is greater and they have certain psychological advantages over the formal media.

Personal Contacts Reach the Undecided

Whenever the respondents were asked to report on their recent exposure to campaign communications of all kinds, political discussions were mentioned more frequently than exposure to radio or print. On any average day, at least 10% more people participated in discussions about the election—either actively or passively—than listened to a major speech or read about campaign items in a newspaper. And this coverage "bonus" came from just those people who had not yet made a final decision as to how they would vote. Political conversations, then, were more likely to reach those people who were still open to influence.

For example, people who made up their minds later in the campaign were more likely to mention personal influences in explaining how they formed their final vote decision. Similarly, we found that the less interested people relied more on conversations and less on the formal media as sources of information. Three-fourths of the respondents who at one time had not expected to vote but were then finally "dragged in" mentioned personal influence. After the election, the voters were given a check list of "sources from which they got most of the information or impressions that caused them to form their judgment on how to vote." Those who had made some change during the campaign mentioned friends or members of their family relatively more frequently than did the respondents who kept a constant vote intention all through the campaign.

The Two-Step Flow of Communications

A special role in the network of personal relationships is played by the "opinion leaders." In Chapter V, we noted that they engaged in political discussion much more than the rest of the respondents. But they reported that the formal media were more effective as sources of influence than personal relationships. This suggests that ideas often flow *from* radio and print *to* the opinion leaders and *from* them to the less active sections of the population.

Occasionally, the more articulate people even pass on an article or point out the importance of a radio speech. Repeatedly, changers referred to reading or listening done under some personal influence. Take the case of a retired school teacher who decided for the Republicans: "The country is ripe for a change

... Willkie is a religious man. *A friend read and highly recom-
mended* Dr. Poling's article in the October issue of the *Chris-
tion Herald* called 'The Religion of Wendell Willkie'."

So much for the "coverage of personal contacts." The person-to-person influence reaches the ones who are more susceptible to change, and serves as a bridge over which formal media
of communications extend their influence. But in addition, personal relationships have certain psychological advantages which
make them especially effective in the exercise of the "molecular
pressures" finally leading to the political homogeneity of social
groups. We turn now to a discussion of five such characteristics.

Non-Purposiveness of Personal Contacts

The weight of personal contacts upon opinion lies, paradoxically, in their greater casualness and non-purposiveness in political matters. If we read or tune in a speech, we usually do so
purposefully, and in doing so we have a definite mental set
which tinges our receptiveness. Such purposive behavior is part
of the broad area of our political experiences, to which we
bring our convictions with a desire to test them and strengthen
them by what is said. This mental set is armor against influence. The extent to which people, and particularly those with
strong partisan views, listen to speakers and read articles with
which they agree in advance is evidence on this point.

On the other hand, people we meet for reasons other than
political discussion are more likely to catch us unprepared, so to
speak, if they make politics the topic. One can avoid newspaper
stories and radio speeches simply by making a slight effort, but
as the campaign mounts and discussion intensifies, it is hard to
avoid some talk of politics. Personal influence is more perva-
sive and less self-selective than the formal media. In short,
politics gets through, especially to the indifferent, much more
easily through personal contacts than in any other way, simply
because it comes up unexpectedly as a sideline or marginal topic
in a casual conversation. For example, there was the restaurant
waitress who decided that Willkie would make a poor president

after first thinking he would be good. Said she: "I had done a little newspaper reading against Willkie, but the real reason I changed my mind was from *hearsay*. So many people don't like Willkie. Many customers in the restaurant said Willkie would be no good." Notice that she was in a position to overhear bits of conversation that were not intended for her. There are many such instances. Talk that is "forbidden fruit" is particularly effective because one need not be suspicious as to the persuasive intentions of the speakers; as a result one's defenses are down. Furthermore, one may feel that he is getting the viewpoint of "people generally," that he is learning how "different people" think about the election.

Such passive participation in conversation is paralleled in the case of the formal media by accidental exposure, e.g., when a political speech is heard because it follows a favorite program. In both conversation and the formal media, such chance communication is particularly effective. And the testimony to such influence is much more frequent in the case of personal contacts. The respondents mentioned it time and again: "I've heard fellows talk at the plant . . . I hear men talk at the shop . . . My husband heard that talked about at work. . ."

Flexibility When Countering Resistance

But suppose we do meet people who want to influence us and suppose they arouse our resistance. Then personal contact still has one great advantage compared with other media: the face-to-face contact can counter and dislodge such resistance, for it is much more flexible. The clever campaign worker, professional or amateur, can make use of a large number of cues to achieve his end. He can choose the occasion at which to speak to the other fellow. He can adapt his story to what he presumes to be the other's interests and his ability to understand. If he notices the other is bored, he can change the subject. If he sees that he has aroused resistance, he can retreat, giving the other the satisfaction of a victory, and come back to his point later. If in the course of the discussion he discovers some pet convictions, he can try to tie up his argument with them. He can spot the moments when the other is yielding, and so time his best punches.

Neither radio nor the printed page can do anything of the kind. They must aim their propaganda shots at the whole target instead of just at the center, which represents any particular individual. In propaganda as much as in other things, one man's meat is another man's poison. This may lead to boomerang effects, when arguments aimed at "average" audiences with "average" reactions fail with Mr. X. The formal media produced several boomerangs upon people who resented what they read or heard and moved in the opposite direction from that intended. But among 58 respondents who mentioned personal contacts as concretely influential, there was only one boomerang. The flexibility of the face-to-face situation undoubtedly accounted for their absence.

Rewards of Compliance

When someone yields to a personal influence in making a vote decision, the reward is immediate and personal. This is not the case in yielding to an argument via print or radio. If a pamphlet argues that voting for the opposite party would be un-American or will jeopardize the future, its warning may sound too remote or improbable. But if a neighbor says the same things, he can "punish" one immediately for being unimpressed or unyielding: he can look angry or sad, he can leave the room and make his fellow feel isolated. The pamphlet can only intimate or describe future deprivations; the living person can create them at once.

Of course all this makes personal contacts a powerful influence only for people who do not like to be out of line. There are certainly some people who gain pleasure from being nonconformists, but under normal circumstances they are probably very much in the minority. Whenever propaganda by another person is experienced as an expression of the prevailing group tendencies, it has greater chances of being successful than the formal media because of social rewards. For example, here is a woman who was for Roosevelt until the middle of the campaign: "I have always been a Democrat and I think Roosevelt has been all right. But my family are all for Willkie. They think he would make the best president and they have been putting the pressure on me." She finally voted for Willkie. This aspect of personal contacts was especially important for women.

The rewards of compliance to other people are learned in early childhood. The easiest way for most children to avoid discomfort is to do what others tell them to do. Someone who holds no strong opinions on politics and hence makes up his mind late in the campaign may very well be susceptible to personal influences because he has learned as a child to take them as useful guides in unknown territory. The young man who was going to vote for Roosevelt because "my grandfather will skin me if I don't" is a case in point.

Trust in an Intimate Source

More people put reliance upon their personal contacts to help them pick out the arguments which are relevant for their own good in political affairs than they do in the more remote and impersonal newspaper and radio. The doubtful voter may feel that the evaluations he reads or hears in a broadcast are plausible, for the expert writer can probably spell out the consequences of voting more clearly than the average citizen. But the voter still wonders whether these are the issues which are really going to affect *his own* future welfare. Perhaps these sources see the problem from a viewpoint entirely different from his own. But he can trust the judgment and evaluation of the respected people among his associates. Most of them are people with the same status and interests as himself. Their attitudes are more relevant for him than the judgments of an unknown editorial writer. In a formal communication the content can be at its best; but in a face to face contact the transference is most readily achieved. For example, here is the case of a young laborer who professed little or no interest in the campaign and who did not even expect to vote until late October: "I've been discussing the election with *the fellows at the shop* and I believe I'll vote, but I haven't decided yet who for." His constant exposure to the views of his fellow-workers not only brought him to the ballot booth but also brought out his final Democratic vote in line with his colleagues.

A middle-aged woman who showed great interest in the campaign was undecided until late October and then voted for Willkie: "*I was talking politics just this morning with a friend, a businessman.* He says business will improve if Willkie is elected and that Willkie promises to keep us out of the war. FDR is getting too much power. He shouldn't have a third term." Her friend had apparently run out for her what amounted to a small catalogue of Republican arguments and he was impressive enough to clinch her vote, which had been in the balance throughout the campaign. Her trust in his judgment settled her mind.

Trust in another person's point of view may be due to his prestige as well as to the plausibility of what he has to say or its relevancy to one's interests. It is obvious that in all influences prestige plays a considerable role. The degree of conformity is greater the higher the prestige of the person in our group who seeks to influence us. The plausibility of the consequences he presents will seem greater if he is important. (Of course, the formal media are also important in this respect.) The heightening of trust through the prestige of certain personal contacts was clear in the case of the driver of a bread truck who changed to Willkie because the prominent president of a business firm had done him the honor of persuading him in that direction. Then, too, there is the case of a middle-aged housewife with little education who was for Willkie from May through September, became undecided in October, and finally voted for Roosevelt. She left Willkie because of the statements of people whom she considered authorities: "I talked with *a college student* from Case, in Cleveland, and students are for Roosevelt because he has helped recreation. I talked, too, with a *man from Chicago who is very interested in politics,* and he doesn't seem to think that Willkie is a big enough man to handle international affairs."

Persuasion Without Conviction

Finally, personal contacts can get a voter to the polls without affecting at all his comprehension of the issues of the election—something the formal media can rarely do. The newspaper or magazine or radio must first be effective in changing attitudes related to the action. There were several clear cases of votes cast not on the issues or even the personalities of the candidates. In fact, they were not really cast for the candidates at all. They were cast, so to speak, for the voters' friends.

"*I was taken to the polls* by a worker who insisted that I go."

"*The lady where I work wanted me to vote.* She took me to the polls and *they all voted Republican so I did too.*"

In short, personal influence, with all its overtones of personal affection and loyalty, can bring to the polls votes that would otherwise not be cast or would be cast for the opposing party just as readily if some other friend had insisted. They differ from the formal media by persuading uninterested people to vote in a certain way without giving them a substantive reason for their vote. Fully 25% of those who mentioned a personal contact in connection with change of mind failed to give a real issue of the campaign as a reason for the change, but only 5% of those who mentioned the formal media omitted such a reason. When personal influence is paramount in this way, the voter is voting mainly for the personal friend, not the candidate.

Practical Implications

In a way the outcome of the election in Erie County is the best evidence for the success of face-to-face contacts. It so happened that for some time the Republican machine in that area worked much more vigorously than its Democratic opponent. When asked whether they knew people who had good ideas about politics, our respondents mentioned considerably more Republican than Democratic local politicians. A few people who did not expect to vote but finally went to the polls mentioned Republican canvassers as the main influence, but we could not trace a similar success for the Democratic machine.

However, one should not identify the personal contacts discussed in this chapter with the efforts of the *professional* political machines. These personal contacts are what one might call *amateur machines* which spring up during elections—individuals who become quite enthusiastic or special groups that try to activate people within their reach. One might almost say that the most successful form of propaganda—especially last-minute propaganda—is to "surround" the people whose vote decision is still dubious so that the only path left to them is the way to the polling booth. We do not know how the budget of the political parties is distributed among different channels of propaganda but we suspect that the largest part of any propaganda budget is spent on pamphlets, radio time, etc. But our findings suggest the task of finding the best ratio between money spent on formal media and money spent on organizing the face-to-face influences, the local "molecular pressures" which vitalize the formal media by more personal interpretation and the full richness of personal relationships into the promotion of the causes which are decided upon in the course of an election.

In the last analysis, more than anything else people can move other people. From an ethical point of view this is a hopeful aspect in the serious social problem of propaganda. The side which has the more enthusiastic supporters and which can mobilize grass-root support in an expert way has great chances of success.

Notes

CHAPTER I

[1] All four groups approximated 600 at the outset. But in any questionnaire study involving repeated interviewing, the problem of "mortality" arises. That is, there are always a few instances in which it is impossible to contact some of the respondents on successive recalls. In this study, mortality arose from a few who refused to be reinterviewed, some who were temporarily unavailable because of illness or travel, and some who moved out of the county permanently or who died. Every effort to keep mortality at a minimum was made. In most cases of difficulty, the field supervisor personally attempted to regain the cooperation of the respondent. In many instances, respondents who were not successfully contacted on one interview were picked up again on the next wave of interviewing. In the panel group, missing cases on the seven interviews were kept down to 14 per cent, a figure which proved to be remarkably low in the experience of subsequent investigators. Analysis of the characteristics of the missing cases showed that the number lost was so small that their influence on the total trends was practically unnoticeable. (Gaudet, Hazel and Wilson, E. C., "Who Escapes the Personal Investigator?" *The Journal of Applied Psychology*, XXIV, December 6, 1940, 773-777.)

[2] Proof that repeated interviewing did not affect the results will be presented in a separate paper.

[3] It is our hope that in all future elections similar studies will be possible. Comparisons over a period of years should greatly enhance the value of any individual results. It is therefore appropriate to add a word here on the kind of improvements which, looking backward, we feel are advisable in such panel studies. Whereas we made seven interviews with our group, in the future it would be sufficient to make four interviews only—one before the conventions, one right after the conventions, one on the eve of the election, and one right after Election Day. The savings so achieved could be used to increase the panel to at least 1,000 cases. There were a number of more refined statistical results which we could not utilize in our study because the necessary cross-tabulations brought us down to too small a number of cases. As far as the interviews with the changers go, a more sophisticated case study technique would be advisable to learn more about the background and the personality of the changers as well as the specific situations in which their changes of mind came about. The reader will find a few specific improvements indicated at

various points throughout the text. Most important of all would be a more detailed study of the role of face-to-face contacts. Furthermore, in the future one should add some more descriptive material on the local campaign as a whole, especially the way the local political committees spent their money and general observations on the behavior of the people at local meetings. Finally, more information on people who were active in the campaign would be useful. In other words, we feel that as far as the voters themselves go, our technique was successful and deserves to be tried out on a broader basis; however, we regret that because of the lack of funds we were not able to supplement it by more information on the specific region in which the campaign went on.

CHAPTER III

[1] Interviewers' ratings actually cover only four steps: A, B, C, and D. Because more than half of the cases fell in the C category, we sub-classified these respondents on the simple question of telephone ownership in order to get a more convenient working distribution. C people with telephones are called C+; C people with no telephones appear as C—.

[2] For a systematic discussion of these ratings, see Genevieve Knupfer, *The Measurement of Socio-Economic Status*, Columbia dissertation, 1943.

[3] See Frederick Mosteller, "The Reliability of Interviewers Ratings" in *Gauging Public Opinion*, Hadley Cantril, editor, Princeton University Press, 1944; also experiments carried out by Archibald Crossley.

[4] See especially *Life's* Continuing Study of Magazine Audiences.

[5] There are many ways in which people can be ranked according to their average status. The average correlation between such indices is about .6. They are usually interchangeable as far as relationships with other variables are concerned. In other words, most of such indices would show the same relationship between socio-economic status and vote.

[6] We use the figure of our May poll for this analysis because of the larger number of cases available. The same result holds for the panel and control groups, separately or in combination, and for each period of the campaign.

[7] The farmers are not included in this classification because they present a special problem. Rural people in this study were much more likely to vote Republican than residents of the urban center of Sandusky.

	PROPORTIONS OF REPUBLICANS		TOTAL WITH DEFINITE VOTE INTENTIONS (MAY)	
	Farmers	Non-Farmers	Farmers	Non-Farmers
A and B	68%	69%	62	276
C+	55	57	89	472
C—	66	42	92	426
D	58	21	38	272

The reader should not be surprised that we have some workers (other than farmers) among the top 17% of the sample, in terms of SES levels. This classification was made in the frame of the prevailing standards of a small town and its rural environment.

There is, of course, a marked correlation between SES levels and type of occupation. On the A and B levels, 80% of the people have "upper" occupations, and on the D level, only 8%. In addition, there are differences within the two occupational groups. On the higher SES levels of the "upper" group we find the professionals, while clerks are found on the lower level of this same group. Similarly, skilled tradesmen are found on the higher SES level of the worker group, while unskilled laborers fall at the lower end of the scale.

[8]The control group was asked the questions in October and the panel group in November. Chart 5 shows the two groups combined.

[9]If this is true, the Catholics in the South would tend to vote more Republican than the southern Protestants. (Such data would test this hypothesis.)

[10]The same result appears if economic status is held constant. In each economic group, the older Protestants are more Republican and the older Catholics are more Democratic. Since education is so bound up with age in this country—the old are less educated than the young because of recent advances in popular schooling—this result may be affected by differences in education. However, the age difference remains even with education held constant (insofar as reliable figures are available).

[11]We have omitted social identification from this correlation because it is not what is usually taken as a primary characteristic, but is rather an attitude derived from such characteristics.

[12]See Appendix B for a detailed description of this index.

CHAPTER IV

[1]Two sets of respondents explained to us their reasons for changing their vote intention. On the one hand there are our panel members. The average time span between the interview and the actual change was two or three weeks. These respondents therefore talked about a rather recent experience. On the other hand there are the control groups, and here the situation is psychologically less satisfactory. In the first control group no explanations for change were asked. The second control group was interviewed in August; three months had elapsed between the two interviews. The third control group was interviewed in October, which meant that some of the changes could reach as far as six months back. Here it is quite likely that considerations developing in the latter phases of the campaign had substituted for original reasons at the time of change. For the main types of arguments (economic reasons, war, third term), it would therefore be unjustified to draw on the counts made with the control groups. There are, indeed, considerable differences in the frequencies with which these arguments appear.

The case is different when it comes to nuances of wording within each area. If a respondent, for instance, chooses to talk about economic reasons and uses a "poor man's argument," there is no reason to assume that the specific selection should be influenced by the time at which his change in vote intention came about. Actually, the specific interrelationships of party and argumentation within one of the major areas turned out to be the same for the panel and the two control groups. We felt justified therefore in including in our tables the two sets of data.

Roughly speaking, we had about an equal number of comments from the panel on the one hand and the two control groups on the other although the one set comes from 600 people and the other from 1,200. There are two reasons for this. One reason is that the interviews with the panel members were done more carefully and therefore the number of comments per interview is larger. Furthermore, the panel contains waverers, that is, people who changed their vote intention at least twice; in the control groups where only two interviews were made with each respondent, no one could register more than one change.

The quotations given in the text are all taken from interviews with panel members.

[2]References to spending and to the national debt might properly be considered indirect attacks upon the works program and other New Deal reform measures, which were vulnerable from the point of view of the expense they involved. However, they were omitted from the class arguments so that the classification would remain fairly rigid. Among the Republicans, such references were nearly two-fifths as numerous as the class arguments and their probable class character should be kept in mind.

[3]Hereafter we shall talk of Republican and Democratic changers to denote the people who made a change favorable to one of the two parties. A Republican change, for example, could involve any one of three steps: from Democrat to Republican; from "undecided" to Republican; or from Democrat to "undecided."

[4]The only exception was the Theodore Roosevelt administration at the beginning of the century. It would be interesting to know how our question would have been answered at that time. Of course we shall never know; but at least it can be hoped that when future elections raise new problems, the social scientist will find reports like the present one useful in retrospect.

[5]The extent to which the careers and identifications of the candidates themselves contributed to this distinction in 1940 is a real question. The point could be tested further by devising several tests ranging from expressions of narrow interests to broad interests. For example, respondents might be asked to indicate the relative prestige which they bestow upon governmental and business personages. Or their reading could be checked, to find out the role of current affairs. Or they could be shown a picture of a large gathering of people and asked to indicate what it meant to them (in the expectation that some would identify it as a political meeting).

[6]For the details on the construction of this index of agreement with either side, see Appendix B: Index of Agreement with Arguments of Either Side.

CHAPTER V

[1]A factor analysis of the different measures of interest and activity will appear in a separate paper.

[2]See Appendix B for detailed description of these indices.

[3]The reader who is interested in statistics is invited to figure out for himself that the age differences would be completely concealed if education were not considered. This can be seen by recomputing the proportion of greatly interested respondents irrespective of educational level.

[4]We use the May poll for this analysis because it gives us larger numbers to work with. The result would be the same, however, if we used only those members of the panel who actually did not vote.

[5]On the whole, our local interviewers as a group were able to identify the residents of Erie County quite well and they agreed that the respondents classified as opinion leaders on our scale were on the whole influential members of their respective social groups.

CHAPTER VI

[1]Throughout this chapter, the degree of interest represented is taken from the first interview. In other words, it is the degree of interest with which the respondent started the campaign. The large majority of respondents maintained their initial level of interest throughout the campaign.

[2]This relationship has a certain correspondence to the psychological "Field Theory" as developed by Kurt Lewin. In developing that theory, Lewin showed, for example, that if a child is acted upon by a psychological force drawing him toward a goal and at the same time acted upon by an equal and opposite force pushing him away from that goal, he would "solve" the problem by moving away from both forces rather than in the direction of either. In other words, the "resultant" leads out of the field.

CHAPTER VII

[1]If a person combined these changes, he was grouped with either the waverers or the party changers. That is, if someone crystallized and then wavered, he was considered a waverer. If he crystallized or wavered and then changed parties, he was considered a party changer.

[2]The data:

	Percentage with Great Interest	Percentage with No or One Cross-Pressure	Total Cases
Constants	43%	79%	196
Indecision waverers	29	71	41
Crystallizers	21	58	109
Party waverers	20	40	15
Party changers	17	33	30

[3]As we go from constants to one-party changers to two-party changers, the factor of cross-pressures becomes relatively more important and the factor of interest less important. As Chart 24 shows (the two middle sections, horizontally, representing the two factors at odds with one another), the ratio of interest to cross-pressures was about 7-to-1 for the constants, 5-to-1 for the one-party changers, and only 2-to-1 for the two-party changers. In other words, the relative strength of the two factors varied: interest was relatively stronger among the constants and cross-pressures relatively stronger among the two-party changers.

CHAPTER VIII

[1]A finer classification of the respondents undecided in May, in terms of their IPP scores, results in the following distribution of the people interviewed in October:

	IPP Score					
October Vote Intention	Strongly Republican	Moderately Republican	Slightly Republican	Slightly Democratic	Moderately Democratic	Strongly Democratic
Republican	9	16	39	10	9	4
Democratic	3	11	18	26	26	12
Total Crystallizers	12	27	57	36	35	16

The result is the same for the control groups interviewed earlier for the second time—one in July and the other in August.

[2]The fact that people select their exposure along the line of their political predispositions is only a special case of a more general law which pervades the whole field of communications research. Exposure is always selective; in other words, a positive relationship exists between people's opinions and what they choose to listen to or read.

In our panel about half the people were constants, i.e., they did not change their vote intention between May and October. The following table shows that the constant Republicans were much more exposed to Republican communications all through this period and Democrats to Democratic communications:

	Predominant Political Color of Exposure			
Vote Intention	Republican	Neutral or None	Democratic	Total
Republican	67%	12%	21%	135
Democratic	23	13	64	95

The interpretation of this result must always be referred back to two sets of factors: a sociological set and a psychological set. Psychologically, at least two elements play a role. It is likely that a desire for reinforcement of one's own point of view exists. This phenomenon is discussed in greater detail at the beginning of Chapter IX. Secondly, it is probably a pleasant experience to read something with which one is familiar if it has not yet reached the stage of boredom. Women's listening to daytime serials would be an example of this. In times of political crisis there seems to be a tendency to listen endlessly to commentators who tell the same story for hours with minor variations. However, these tendencies—toward reassurance and toward interest in familiar material—deserve further study.

On one hand we have the sifting of communications by the environment, as was pointed out in the text. In addition, we have here a phenomenon of group solidarity. Most people read newspapers in order to read the daily news, the sport page, the comics, etc. In most newspapers this material is the same but a Republican will prefer to get such material from a Republican newspaper as a sort of symbol that he belongs to his own political group. In times of a presidential campaign, when the newspapers start to take definite views on current events, the two groups then find themselves more and more exposed to the arguments of their own side; it is not certain whether they would not be more willing to accept a more balanced supply of communications if it were not for the inertia of their sticking to the newspapers they habitually subscribe to. The latter point could be proven if one were to show that the exposure bias is greater with newspaper reading than with radio listening; our own material is not extensive enough to permit such a test.

It is possible, incidentally, that this phenomenon of inertia in newspaper reading also accounts for at least part of the deviate cases, the people who are more exposed to the propaganda of the enemy party. These seem to be partly people who by coincidence get their daily news from a newspaper of the opposite color and then in times of election do not bother to change. In regard to radio, most of the exposure to the speeches of the enemy seems to come from people who in general are not much interested in listening to political radio programs and tune in only if the candidates themselves talk. This, of course, makes for a more balanced diet.

The latter point would help to explain a noticeable refinement of our main result. We can divide people according to their interest in the campaign into two groups, those on the highest and those on the two lower interest levels. Communication bias is stronger with the more interested people (see Chart 30). This result, however, has a very complex nature. Interested people, as we have seen, are more likely to be biased in their exposure; but biased exposure probably also heightens interest. This result, too, deserves further study. It is obviously of great practical importance that the more deeply involved people are in a political point of view, the more they shut themselves off from ideas which might invite argument and reconsideration.

[3]Actually, coming to a decision itself results in increased exposure. A campaign is more like an exciting football game than like a deep-probing research. The voter who has decided is not out of the game—he is just getting in. For most Americans the rivalry of the contest overshadows the personal quest

to decide on which side to play. (See Chapter XIII for an account of the contest element in campaign communications.) So it comes about that the voter's interest and zeal for political endeavor rises *after* his personal decision has been made. The big action lies ahead. Zest mounts up to the hour when the returns come in.

To show the effect of having a vote intention upon exposure, let us compare the exposure scores for the second half of the campaign for those who had a vote intention in August and those who did not. (In other words, compare the first and second lines in the following table). The table shows that those who had a vote intention (first line) exposed themselves to more propaganda than those who did not. This comparison is carried through in four different groups in order to control the amount of exposure during the first part of the campaign. On each level of exposure those who had made up their minds by August had a higher average exposure score for September-November than those who had not yet formed their vote intention by August. By the same procedure, we can show that having vote intention affects the degree of interest in the election in the same way.

	AVERAGE EXPOSURE SCORES SEPTEMBER-NOVEMBER —*Exposure May-August*—				TOTAL CASES —*Exposure May-August*—			
	High	Moderate	Limited	Low	High	Moderate	Limited	Low
Definite vote intention in August	16.9	11.7	8.4	4.8	100	119	122	48
No definite vote intention in August	14.7	9.4	6.8	3.0	13	14	37	53

CHAPTER IX

[1]Such partisan exposure is not confined to politics. Its application to other areas of communication has also been established. For example, educational broadcasts reach primarily those people who need them least; in a recent series of program on the contributions of various national minorities to American life, the audience for each program was primarily composed of the members of the particular minority group being extolled. Such exposure even extends to commercial communications; people tend to read advertisements of the things they already own and listen to the radio programs sponsored by the company which manufactures their most important possessions.

[2]This represents only an extension of what we saw in operation in the case of activation, where people undecided in vote selected communications which fit their political predispositions. Here, however, this is intensified because not only predispositions (in most cases) but also vote preference makes for the selection of partisan communications.

CHAPTER X

[1]The average exposure score for those with a constant political preference was 10.9; the "non-constants" had an average exposure score of 9.3.

[2]The data:

	GENERAL EXPOSURE SEPTEMBER TO NOVEMBER			
Exposure Bias	Very high	Medium high	Medium low	Very low
Exposed predominantly to propaganda of own side	66%	63%	55%	53%
Balanced or no exposure	11	11	14	11
Exposed predominantly to propaganda of other side	23	26	31	36
Total cases	122	117	107	47

CHAPTER XI

[1]Louis Bean, *Ballot Behavior*, American Council on Public Affairs, 1940.

[2]We might also follow the partial conversions through another change in order to discover the ultimate effect of the campaign upon them. As we have seen, most of those who leave the party appropriate for their IPP later return to it; they would then be re-converted and reinforced. Similarly, those who leave a vote intention counter to their IPP usually end up with a vote intention consistent with it; they would then be reconverted. In other words, only a small group of the partial conversions would finally be classified as real conversions.

CHAPTER XII

[1]These correlations are based on the 1,200 cases interviewed in October, omitting those who had neither an expectation of the winner nor a vote intention. At that time there were not enough people on the lowest interest level to permit the computation of a third correlation coefficient.

[2]In general, voters decide in line with their IPP, but expectation affects vote intention even when differences of IPP are controlled. A respondent with a Republican IPP was more likely to vote Republican if he expected Willkie to win than if he expected Roosevelt to win.

	———NO VOTE INTENTION IN MAY———			
	REPUBLICAN IPP		DEMOCRATIC IPP	
October Vote Intention	Republican expectation	Democratic expectation	Republican expectation	Democratic expectation
Republican	9	16	4	3
Democratic	6	16	8	27

[3]We have seen that there is a generally high correlation between expectation as to winner and vote intention. Two psychological processes can account for this relationship. One is the bandwagon effect discussed in the text. Here expectation influences vote intention. However, there is also the possibility of "projection"; people may project their own vote intention on others and expect them to behave in the way they themselves behave. In that case the correlation would be explained by expectation's being the consequence of vote intention. A finer statistical analysis shows that both processes—bandwagon effect and projection—play a role, but that the former is constantly the more important. The evidence is given in a paper on "The Analysis of the Mutual Interaction of Two Correlated Factors," which will be published separately.

CHAPTER XIII

[1]For an elaboration of this chapter see Douglas Waples and Bernard Berelson, *Public Communications and Public Opinion*, Chicago, mimeographed, 1941. Particular credit is due Dr. Waples for his competent supervision of the analytic work reported in this chapter. The contributions of Dr. N. C. Leites and Mr. Ithiel Pool are also acknowledged.

[2]The analysis includes parts of 28 major radio speeches by the candidates and their supporters as well as some newscasts over local stations. In magazines, the analysis covered the campaign material in seven of the most widely read magazines in the county—*Life, Colliers, Liberty, Saturday Evening Post, Reader's Digest, Time* and *Look*; in all, 64 magazine editorials or articles were sampled. The newspaper analysis, totaling 158 items, included the front-page stories on the campaign and the political columnists (Walter Lippmann, Dorothy Thompson, Paul Mallon, Jay Franklin, Ray Tucker) in the four major papers. Within these limits, and the time periods indicated in the text, the analysis covered everything dealing with the campaign, whether directly concerned with the "issues" or not.

CHAPTER XIV

[1]We have evidence to show, in fact, that exposure to campaign materials was higher at this period than at any other. At various times during the campaign, the respondents:

(a) were asked which of a list of five major political talks broadcast in the preceding interval they had heard;

(b) were shown the front page of the preceding day's issue of the newspaper which they reported reading regularly and were asked which of the stories dealing with the campaign they had read; and

(c) were shown a list of campaign articles which appeared in the mass magazines and were asked to indicate which they had read.

The figures in the following table represent the proportion of respondents who were exposed to at least one item in the media.

Time of Interview	MEDIUM EXPOSED TO:		
	Radio	Newspaper	Magazine
July (between conventions)	42%	29%	17%
September	28	*	21
October	54	51	26

*Question not asked.

[2]In order to discriminate between "high" and "low" exposure groups, indices of exposure were developed on the basis of all available communication data pertaining to the panel group. These indices provide composite scores for each respondent indicating the relative amount of political material read in newspapers and magazines and heard on the radio. It was also possible in this way to determine general exposure to all sources for the campaign as a whole, for the early months (May through August)and for the last two months prior to the election. For details on the construction of these indices, see Appendix B.

[3]This same pattern of overlapping exposure obtained for each of the three public media of communication. Most of the people who were exposed to political items in the newspaper at one time were also exposed at another. The same relationship holds for exposure to radio and magazine material.

[4]The data:

	Average Exposure Scores	Total Cases
SOME HIGH SCHOOL OR MORE:		
Men	11.5	156
Women	10.2	183
45 and over	11.8	99
Under 45	10.4	240
Urban	11.2	179
Rural	10.3	134
A, B	13.3	54
C+	10.3	110
C—	10.3	106
D	9.6	43
Great interest	12.3	142
Medium interest	9.2	138
No interest	7.7	9
Has a definite vote intention	11.0	261
Doesn't know for whom to vote	9.0	16
Doesn't expect to vote	7.9	24

No High School:

Men	9.8	111
Women	7.7	113
45 and over	9.1	158
Under 45	8.3	66
Urban	8.8	128
Rural	9.2	96
A, B	10.5	23
C+	9.0	60
C—	8.4	73
D	8.1	68
Great interest	10.9	45
Medium interest	8.4	136
No interest	5.7	24
Has a definite vote intention	9.5	153
Doesn't know for whom to vote	7.4	11
Doesn't expect to vote	6.3	45

[5]Let us recall the newspaper situation in Erie County at this point. There were three newspapers in Sandusky with wide distribution throughout the county. In addition, the *Cleveland Plain Dealer* was read by a considerable number of residents of the county. For a county of this sort, such newspaper opportunities are exceptionally good. Of course, they might be still better in the metropoli of the country.

[6]For an analysis covering this point, see "Biographies in Popular Magazines," by Leo Lowenthal, in *Radio Research, 1942-1943*, edited by Paul F. Lazarsfeld and Frank N. Stanton, New York, 1944, p. 507-548.

CHAPTER XV

[1]The statement that people vote in groups is not very satisfactory. People belong to a variety of groups and therefore further research is necessary on the question: with *which group* are they most likely to vote? The approximate procedure will be to select a sample of people and to take an inventory of the groups they belong to. There will be the family, co-workers, family associates, neighbors and groups of people "they go with." For each respondent we shall need a list of the people who form these groups and their vote intentions.

As the first result we will have a measure of political homogeneity of the different types of groups. This might be called an extension of the sociometric method in social research.

The rank order of the different groups, in terms of the influence they exert on the respondent, need not be the same for each individual. Some people might wish to conform to their business associates and others to their neighbors. As a next step it will therefore be advisable to look for persons who find themselves at the point of intersection of two or more groups with different political majorities. In specific case studies, we would try to find out to what extent the people are aware of the conflict and by what criteria they make their decision. In all these studies, objective definitions of the different groups would of course be necessary.

In our study we do not have refined data on this point. But as a substitute one might consider the following information. In the final interview, a list of sources which might possibly have been influential in determining a vote was submitted to the respondents:

"From which of these sources did you get most of the information or impressions that caused you to form your judgment on how to vote: relatives, business contacts or fellow workers, other friends or neighbors, public speakers (not radio), personal visit of the candidate, party worker in person, telephone call from party worker, party literature, newsreels, magazines, radio, newspapers? Which of the ones selected were most important to you?"

The following table shows specifically for men and women how often the three possibilities of relatives, friends, and business acquaintances were mentioned, either as one of several influences or as the most important one.

	Men	*Women*
INFLUENTIAL:*		
Relatives	5%	33%
Business contacts	33	8
Friends and neighbors	14	23
No mention of personal contact as source	56	52
MOST IMPORTANT:		
Relatives	**	14
Business contacts	19	5
Friends and neighbors	4	6
No mention of personal contact as source	77	75
Total Voters	215	198

*The "influential" group adds to more than 100 per cent because each voter could have named more than one specific kind of personal contact.

**Less than one-half of one per cent.

A similar comparison reveals the differences between business and professional people, workers, and farmers:

	White Collar Workers	Manual Workers	Farmers
INFLUENTIAL:			
Relatives	5%	8%	8%
Business contacts	38	41	8
Friends and neighbors	8	17	25
No mention of personal contact as source	57	47	70
MOST IMPORTANT:			
Relatives	3	1	3
Business contacts	17	28	5
Friends and neighbors	1	4	10
No mention of personal contact as source	79	67	82
Total Voters	76	96	40

*The "influential" group adds to more than 100 per cent because each voter could have named more than one specific kind of personal contact.

[2]This tendency toward consistency of opinion and predisposition is discussed more fully in a later section of this chapter.

[3]The data:

	DIRECTION OF VOTE CHANGE	
IPP	Democratic to Republican	Republican to Democratic
Republican	8	3
Democratic	8	10

[4]Included among those who observed no changes are those few respondents who saw changes in both directions. In each group, however, these constitute no more than 10% of the total "none" response. Including these, then, 44% of the Republicans, 61% of the Democrats, and 72% of those with no definite preference said that they noticed no changes of vote intention in the people around them. These differences may be explained thus: that (a) Democrats, on the whole, were less well educated than Republicans, and were therefore less conscious of such changes, and (b) people who have no particular preference are not only less interested in making such observations, but in addition, are probably surrounded by people who themselves are less likely to change.

[5]In November there were a few dubious cases where we were not sure whether people restricted themselves to the members of the same household or referred to relatives not living with them in answering this question. This is due to the fact that in August respondents were asked to specify the vote intention of each family member, whereas in November we only asked the general question "Did anyone in your family vote differently from you?"

From subsequent check-ups we are satisfied that the uncertainty could not have changed the results by more than 1% in either direction.

[6]The data:

SES Level	Proportions Belonging to Organizations	Total Cases
A, B	72%	158
C+	56	336
C—	44	353
D	35	204

[7]A paper to be published separately on "The Analysis of the Mutual Interaction of Two Correlated Factors" goes into this problem in detail.

CHAPTER XVI

[1]In two respects it is more difficult to get an index of personal exposure as compared with one of radio listening and newspaper reading. One involves a memory factor. Radio speeches are rather distinct events and people are not likely to listen to too many of them. Therefore if they are asked to remember those they have been exposed to, they are bound not to make too many mistakes. With newspapers it is still simpler because we can place the entire paper before them and their recognition is fairly reliable, as we have seen in various studies using this method. But people meet people the whole day long, and it is not nearly so likely that they can remember everything that passed between them in discussion. At least it would first be necessary to do some experimentation with personal contact diaries as suggested in the text.

To this we have to add the element of self-consciousness. If people know that they have to keep a record of what they talked about with other people, they might very well be affected in their selection of topic. Radio diaries have been tested and it seems that keeping such diaries make people record their radio diet substantially. But this might be due to the fact that radio listening is a much more standardized pursuit; talking with people is much more flexible and might therefore be more affected by a request for systematic recording.

It is hoped that experimentation in this direction will be furthered.

Construction of Indices

At many points in the text we referred to indices which we had formed to help us study political predispositions, activities, and attitudes. The following is a brief explanation of each of these indices.

THE INDEX OF POLITICAL PREDISPOSITION (IPP)

A study of the voters showed that the three factors with the best predictive value for vote were religion, SES level, and residence. This index was formed by stratifying within each SES level for religion and residence. A wealthy Protestant farmer got an IPP score of 1, and this meant he had a strong Republican predisposition. A Catholic on the lowest SES level, living in the urban center of Erie County, was rated 7, and this meant he had a strong Democratic predisposition. The scoring procedure:

| | PROTESTANT | | CATHOLIC | |
	Rural	Urban	Rural	Urban
A, B	1	2	3	4
C+	2	3	4	5
C—	3	4	5	6
D	4	5	6	7

Following is the distribution of the respondents in May according to this index:

Score	Frequency	
1	148	Predominantly
2	289	Republican
3	467	Predispositions
4	319	Predominantly
5	283	Democratic
6	97	Predispositions
7	47	

THE INDEX OF POLITICAL ACTIVITY

Participation in the campaign was measured by combining the answers to the following questions:

"Have you tried to convince anyone of your political ideas recently?"

	Score	Frequency
Yes	2	74
DK	1	1
No	0	429

"Have you done anything to help get your candidate elected?"

Yes	2	69
DK	2	1
No	0	424

"Which of the following statements corresponds most closely to your feeling about the election?"

"I am very anxious to see my candidate elected"	2	301
"I would like to see him win, but it is not terribly important to me"	1	117
"It doesn't make much difference to me who wins"	0	86

The scores inserted after each of the possible responses indicate the contributions they make to the participation index. A score of six represents the highest degree of political interest and activity and a score of zero signifies almost complete indifference.

THE INDEX OF BREADTH OF OPINION

During the course of the study, many questions of current public interest were posed to the respondents to determine their stands. There were always some people who had no opinion. This is what the index tries to get at. We do not care here which view they held for the purpose of determining their breadth of opinion, but only *whether* they held a view.

We used five such questions put to the panel group and five that had been put to the control group. If a respondent expressed an opinion on all five questions, he got a score of five. Every time he said "Don't know," he lost a point. The score for each respondent gives us insight into his "breadth of opinion."

Following were the questions used:

THE PANEL

"Which do you think is more important—a president who is capable of dealing with the European situation or one who is capable of dealing with our economic problems at home?"

"How do you feel about the passage of the conscription bill—do you approve or disapprove?"

"How do you feel about President Roosevelt running for a third term—do you approve, disapprove, or doesn't it matter to you?"

"At the present time, what should the United States do about helping England?"

"What do you think of unions on the whole—are they a good thing or a bad thing?"

THE CONTROL

"Which do you think is more important—a president who is capable of dealing with the European situation or one who is capable of dealing with our economic problems at home?"

"What kind of a president do you think Roosevelt has made—good, fair or no good?"

"How do you feel about President Roosevelt running for a third term—do you approve, disapprove or doesn't it matter to you?"

"What kind of a president do you think Willkie would make—good, fair or no good?"

"If you had to choose for president between a man who has had mostly experience in government and a man who has had mostly experience in business, which would you choose?"

THE INDEX OF MAGAZINE READING ON THE CAMPAIGN

The respondent was asked about several specific articles appearing in current issues of magazines. This index is simply a count of the number of articles on political affairs that the respondent reported reading.

THE INDEX OF NEWSPAPER READING ON THE CAMPAIGN

Interviewers asked about the respondents' newspaper reading habits. How frequently did they read the various columnists available in local papers? How many front page articles on the election did they recognize? Did they read about the conventions in the newspaper? The greater such newspaper reading activity, the higher the score describing exposure to political material in newspapers.

THE INDEX OF RADIO LISTENING ON THE CAMPAIGN

Respondents were asked whether they had listened to specific radio speeches. They got a positive score every time they answerd affirmatively. They were also queried about listening to the political conventions and to political speeches in general. Every answer indicating attention to political material over the radio contributed to a high "political radio listening" score.

THE INDEX OF GENERAL OR OVER-ALL EXPOSURE TO THE CAMPAIGN

The general exposure index is merely a summation of the specific indices we formed to show the number of magazine articles read, the extent of reading about political material and other news items in the newspapers, the amount of listening to political and other news on the radio, and the degree of exposure to newsreels, to political discussions, and to public meetings. A simple average of the separate indices yielded the general exposure index.

Questions of the following types were included in these indices:

"How much did you read about it (the Republican National Convention, the Democratic National Convention) in the newspapers—quite a bit, only a little, only the headlines, or not at all?"

"Did you read the article in ——(magazine)—— on —————— recently?"

"How frequently do you listen to news broadcasts over the radio—frequently, occasionally or never? Do you usually turn the news on of your own accord or does someone else turn it on?"

"Did you hear —————— speak over the radio recently?"

"Have you heard anyone (family or friends) discussing national politics since we were here before?"

"Did you see Willkie when he spoke at the railroad station?"

"Which of these front-page newspaper stories on the election did you read yesterday?"

"Do you listen to political speeches over the radio during political campaigns: a great deal, sometimes, rarely or never?"

"With whom have you talked recently about national politics?"

"How often do you usually attend the movies? Did you see the following newsreels?"

"Which do you talk about more with your family (friends)—the political campaign or the war?"

Each answer which revealed that the respondent had read or listened to political communications gave him a higher score than one which revealed that he had not been exposed to such communications. We can determine general exposure in this way for two periods of the campaign—from May to August and from September to November.

THE INDEX OF POLITICAL EXPOSURE BIAS

This index is designed to indicate whether the respondent was exposed to predominantly Republican or Democratic material. For the purposes of this index, it was necessary to study the political content of the speeches listened to and the magazine and newspaper articles read.

The respondent was arbitrarily given a positive score for every item favoring the Republicans and a negative score for every item of Democratic flavor that he had read or heard. If he heard speeches by Roosevelt or Wallace or Ickes, or read an article praising the New Deal in a magazine or newspaper, or reported listening to or reading about the Democratic National Convention, his exposure score tended toward the Democrats. If, on the other hand, he listened to Willkie or John L. Lewis, or read the editorials of a Republican newspaper, or heard or read about the Republican Convention, he got a positive score indicating a Republican tendency. The summation of all such scores disclosed the political color of the respondent's exposure.

This index was composed separately for each of the main campaign periods: once for the convention period (between May and August) and again for the period between September and November.

INDEX OF AGREEMENT WITH ARGUMENTS OF EITHER SIDE

In the October interview, each respondent was asked whether he agreed with the following eight arguments then current in the campaign:

"Roosevelt has great personal attractiveness, capacity for hard work, and keen intelligence."

"Willkie is a self-made small-town man, who made his way by his genius for industrial organization."

"Willkie is a corporation lawyer whose real sympathies are all with big business."

"The New Deal has interfered too much with private business."

"Roosevelt is rushing the country into war against most of the rest of the world."

"We should not break the democratic tradition by electing any president to a third term."

"With Roosevelt as president, the United States is less likely to yield to Hitler."

"Willkie will increase production by gaining the confidence of business."

If a voter agreed with an argument supporting his own side or disagreed with an argument supporting the opposition, he received a +1 score. If he disagreed with his own argument or agreed with the opposition's, he received a —1 score. Indecision on any argument was scored as zero. Thus each respondent could score theoretically from +8 to —8. The 25% in complete or nearly complete agreement scored from +6 to +8. The 35% of lukewarm respondents scored from +1 to —5.